THE GIRL
FROM
LAMAHA
STREET

THE GIRL FROM FROM LAMAHA STREET

SHARON MAAS

Thread

Published by Thread in 2022

An imprint of Storyfire Ltd.
Carmelite House
50 Victoria Embankment
London EC4Y 0DZ

www.thread-books.com

ISBN: 978-1-80019-725-1
eBook ISBN: 978-1-80019-723-7

In memory of the great women in my life who have passed on:
Granny Mirri, Granny Winnie, Mum, Aunt Leila

Granny Mirri lived in the Lamaha Street house that became my first real nest, with her mostly silent and immobile presence at its core. The house, like most Georgetown houses of the time, was of wood, painted white, and built on high pillars. It was a typical old Dutch Colonial residence: a five-bedroom, many-windowed house, with an outside staircase leading up to the front door, and the 'bottom house' between the concrete stilts providing a garage, storage rooms and open spaces.

The wide front room, which we called the gallery, was nothing *but* window, alternating glass and wooden louvres, while traditional Demerara windows, known to us as 'coolers', opened up the house sides and the top storey. Demerara windows were ornately carved, open-topped wooden boxes jutting out from the house, closed off by slanting wooden shutters. In the old days, before electric fans took over, people placed big blocks of ice in the window boxes to cool the incoming breeze – an ingenious and simple method of air conditioning.

The house on Lamaha Street

To me, Granny was always old, sitting in the gallery in the chair of honour, overlooking Lamaha Street, her thinning white hair tied back in a bun at the nape of her neck, the loose skin of her hands and arms gossamer-thin, like soft, transparent silk, her generous bosom a soft cushion to nestle against. I have no memory of her ever on her feet. She just sat there, all day, supposedly escorted there early every morning by Aunt Leila (pronounced Lee-la), and back upstairs to bed every evening. She couldn't have been all that old, mid-sixties at most, but to little me, she was ancient, and my rock.

Granny Mirri spent her entire day in the worn-out Morris chair next to the gallery window. Nothing recalls lazy colonial British Guiana leisure time like the Morris, the first adjustable-back-recliner dating back to 1865 and William Morris's English firm. The Morris chair conjures up visions of wealthy British sugar planters relaxing after a day's work in the scorching sun, coming home in the cool of the evening to enjoy a rum sizzler on the veranda; sprawled on the Morris, legs up. It's a wide, comfortable armchair, with flat, wooden armrests you can set a glass or even a plate on. The armrests have extensions tucked neatly beneath them that fold out into leg- and footrests. The backrest is adjustable, using two pegs inserted into holes in the arms, so that the whole chair can be inclined back to various horizontal levels. A chair to doze in. I expect that's what those planters did, while barefoot Black boys padded back and forth, filling their glasses.

But for Granny Mirri it was her place. Her home-within-a-home. Next to her, on the windowsill, stood a bottle of pale-yellow Limacol.

Limacol: the Freshness of a Breeze in a Bottle was its slogan, and indeed it was: an astringent with a thousand uses. You could splash your face with it on hot days and its sharp coolness would shock new life into you. Men used it as an aftershave, women as a make-up remover or even a deodorant. Limacol was a staple in every Guiana

Chapter Four

Eileen and David

Granny Mirri had four children. Actually, she had five, but one, a boy named Walter, died in childhood after a tragic fall. Three girls remained, Leila, Elma and Eileen, and another boy, Percy, who was the baby of the family.

My mother, Eileen Rosaline Cox, born in January 1918, was the third child and youngest girl. The Cox family lived in that white wooden two-storeyed house on Lamaha Street in Georgetown, the capital of British Guiana, which now seems like a mythical country. British, because it was still a colony back then, and Guiana because it's a part of the Guiana Shield, a 1.7-billion-year old Precambrian geological formation on the north-east coast of South America. Mythical, because British Guiana no longer exists. It is now Guyana, an independent nation. It's a different state of being.

Back then, we called our country BeeGee, in writing shortened to BG. The very word BG, to many of us who were there, evokes a deeply comforting, sweetly mellow sense of nostalgia. Britain's seemingly benign hand held us safe and cosy, and as long as you didn't think too deeply about the implications, you basked in the comfiness of it all. Many of us who grew up in this benign atmosphere were like children, coddled in mothers' arms. The mellow spirit of BG seeped into a child's being, whispered in a child's ear and folded its arms around a child's soul. We share the inimitable *feel* of BG, and that's the atmosphere Eileen knew as a child. On the surface, she had a happy childhood, with loving parents and beloved siblings. A calm, settled and conventional young life, without much in the way of conflict and struggle. Superficially at least, all was well in her middle-class world, in those halcyon days of Crown and colony.

But there was another reality to life in BG, a dark reality. There were others who lived out of public sight: workers on the sugar estates toiling dawn to dusk in the blistering sun or sweating in the factories and dockyards, victims of a cruel system that exploited their only asset: their labour. It was easy to forget their existence, to wallow in one's own privilege of birth, or fight to raise oneself even higher in the class system, to ignore the pain and suffering of those less fortunate.

But Eileen was of a different calibre, one of the few who couldn't ignore or forget those in the shadows, or wallow smugly in her own good fortune, blind to that other reality. She was one of the few who peeked beyond her own little bubble of well-being, and from a young age what she saw disturbed her. How could she be happy when swathes of her countrymen lived in poverty, exploited to the limit so that others could live in comfort? She felt the call of destiny, and answered it without a moment's hesitation.

Back then, in the late 1940s, early 50s, the highest ambition of most girls was to quickly put boring education behind them, meet the perfect man, marry him, and raise the perfect family in the perfect home. But not for Eileen. She had a vision, a calling. She grew up to attend the selective Bishops' High School, the country's top state school for girls, and by the end of her schooldays had made a name for herself as best student and head girl, a candidate for the national scholarship, which would have enabled her to attend university in England. But she withdrew from the competition.

'Why?' I asked her later, much later. 'Why didn't you accept it? Why did you withdraw? You would have been brilliant. You could have studied law, or economics.'

'I wanted to work for people and with people,' she told me. 'I didn't want book-learning. I wanted to work from a grassroots level.'

'But with a degree you could have come back home,' I said. 'You could have had a leading position. You would have been a minister, perhaps. You could even have been prime minister. You could have had influence, power. You could have changed society.'

She only smiled. 'These high-up people in positions of so-called power still have to play by the rules. They are limited in what they can do. They are all party politicians, toeing the line, bowing to authorities above them. They all dance to puppetmasters. And they are corruptible. Power becomes personal. Even good people change when power falls into their hands. I didn't want that. I knew I could do far more from beneath than from above. And some of them who study abroad never come back from the greener pastures. They seek the good life for themselves.'

Her calling was right here, at home, and it did not involve marriage. Back then, there were few career opportunities for a girl in British Guiana, but there were jobs, and many girls became teachers, nurses, secretaries and clerks. They worked in the civil service, in banks and insurance companies and local businesses, jobs that were stopgaps between school and marriage. But Eileen stayed resolutely single.

She was actually a good 'catch', for she and her sisters belonged to the strata of society called 'coloured middle class'; that is, she was of mixed race, with identifiably English, meaning white, family members in her direct lineage, and quite fair herself. This placed her fairly high in a hierarchy in which skin colour was the main criterion – along with a family's reputation and social standing, education, employment, white ancestry.

The three Cox girls were all fair-skinned, respectable girls of a solid middle-class family, the next best thing to being actually white, their 'hard' hair the only thing that revealed their mixed race. Mum would have caught many a young man's eye, being pretty in a neat, effortless, artless sort of way. But in her case, her intelligence, education and work ethic would have been black

Mummy and me, on the front stairs of the Lamaha Street house

marks against her, scaring away potential suitors. No man wanted a woman who argued with him as a wife, one with ideas of her own about marriage and her role in it. Her behaviour, indeed, must have been puzzling and off-putting to suitors.

Instead of putting herself on the marriage market, upon leaving school Eileen learned shorthand and typing and joined the British Guiana civil service. With above-average secretarial skills, she did well, but then, everything she did was above average. Whether it was French or Latin or maths or science or simply handwriting, she was the best, and so it was in the civil service. She began to slowly work her way up. It was good to earn her own money, not be dependent on a husband.

At one point in her twenties she did get engaged. But her fiancé broke it off when she announced that she was planning to continue working after marriage. For a young woman in the civil service, getting married meant she'd have to quit her job, and she had no intention of doing so. She shrugged him off, stayed single, and approached her thirtieth birthday wearing that cruel label of 'old maid'. But she wore it with dignity and nonchalance. She'd caught the heady taste of independence; she did not need a man.

Then she met David, the man who would become my father. He was a tall, dark and very handsome young man, not only of sharp intelligence but, like her, with a highly developed social conscience and unconventionally independent political opinions. A man with a mind of his own, a heart – like hers – open to the underdog, as well as charm, humour and impeccable manners. A man of compassion, ready and willing to fight for the rights of others, just as she was. He wooed her, and, accepting her conditions, won her. Considering her criteria, David must have been quite extraordinary. Who was he, then?

David Hamilton Westmaas, the second of Granny Winnie's eight sons, was born in 1914 to a family that already had quite a reputation for non-conformity and rebellion. It all started with Granny Winnie, a fair-skinned woman of almost (but not quite!) pure English lineage. Defying her parents' wishes, she had married a dark-skinned man of the coloured middle class, several notches down the racial hierarchy from her. At the time, that was just Not the Done Thing. Women had to marry 'up'; class and race were everything. Winnie defied that 'everything'. She married her George Westmaas, and proceeded to give birth to and raise her eight sons.

David, like all his brothers, attended Queen's College, the colony's elite secondary school for boys, after which he joined the British Guiana civil service in 1933, first as a clerical assistant at the deeds registry and medical department, and finally as a clerk at the customs department. In the meantime – probably due to the rumblings of a distant war across the ocean – he served with both the British Guiana Militia and the British Guiana regiment, and taught courses in the use of Vickers machine guns and Bren guns

Seven Westmaas brothers. Daddy is far left, next to him Uncle Denis, with a toy rifle. Uncle Rory, the baby, still too young for the photo

as part of the local preparation for war. When the Second World War broke out, he volunteered to fight against Nazi Germany along with three of his brothers and many more of his countrymen. Called up, he served with the RAF in England. He returned home after the war, alive and unharmed but forever changed.

Back in BG, he returned to public service and worked over the next few years in several departments, including the Ministries of Lands and Mines, and Agriculture. That's when, and perhaps where, he met Eileen Cox, a woman who at over thirty years of age was no longer young, and in fact already wore that ugly label of old maid. He married her in 1950.

Their wedding photo shows a handsome couple. Mum is slim, trim and well groomed in a sensible, rather masculine, tailored jacket, and holds an unpretentious bouquet at her waist. I imagine she's wearing sensible flat shoes; I've never seen her in high heels, or any glamorous shoes (or clothes) at all. Her smile is candid, confident, relaxed. No overflowing emotions here, no delighted smiles and tears of joy, no frothy veil, no long white wedding gown, no walking down the aisle. She wears no make-up beyond (presumably) her favourite moisturiser at the time, coconut oil, and, perhaps a pat of face powder. Her hair is in its signature style, parted slightly off-centre, and tucked into a neat bun at the nape of her neck. She has a high forehead; she's brainy.

Wedding photo: my parents

It was a register office wedding. Mum, practical and sensible as ever, had no time or patience for a weepy white church wedding, and besides, she was an agnostic, and the man she married was an atheist. Of course they wouldn't marry in church!

Eileen and David shared a highly developed social conscience, a determination to work for the betterment of their country. They were, superficially at least, well suited. But in Mum's case, 'working for the betterment of her country' meant, first and foremost, working for the improvement of women's lot. That began with herself. It was no accident that she was still a spinster at the age of thirty. Eileen had from the start, along with other women in public life, been fighting a legal battle for progress. By the time she signed that register, she had already achieved her first victory in the fight for women's rights: the right for a married woman to stay on at her civil service job. And so she set off on her marital journey as a working wife.

By this time Eileen already owned her own home. Years earlier, she had bought, with her savings, a building site in a residential development on the outskirts of Georgetown, a coastal area just past Kitty Village along the Atlantic coastline. This was Subryanville, a green, breezy area where middle-class families could put down roots just a few minutes' walk from the Sea Wall.

She was among the first to claim one of the coveted house lots, and so hers was on First Avenue, closest to the ocean, a prime location. She bought high-quality greenheart wood from the demolished former Bishops' High School building, and with that, she built the breezy wooden house that was to become her first marital home, and my own very first home as a baby and toddler.

It was a one-storey house on tall stilts. Its ocean-facing front aspect was all windows, and when they were open the cool sea breeze swept through the house, brushing through all the rooms, which had no ceilings, to allow for ventilation. It had two large bedrooms and a kitchen overlooking a backyard with several fruit trees. It was a house of space and light, with a direct view of the Atlantic. And it was all hers.

And so, in a reversal of tradition, David moved into his wife's home, and they started a family: me. I was born a year later, in 1951, when she was thirty-three: geriatric, for a first-time mother of her day. Daddy, who loved all things Russian, wanted to name me Olga. Thank goodness, Mummy put her foot down.

Eileen, David, and their baby: me

Chapter Five

Small Days

I was a rebellious baby. My first rebellion wrecked Mum's carefully laid out plan of going back to work full-time after having me. By this time, Mum had been working her way up through the civil service for many years. She had no intention of giving up that prized job, just as she hadn't given it up for marriage. Returning to paid work was a scandalous thing for a 50s wife and mother, but she had a destiny to follow, and follow it she did. Now, she'd devised a plan as to how to have both a baby and a working life. Yet her work was not a career in today's sense of the word. If she'd wanted a career, she'd have taken that scholarship she was offered, an avenue to high rank. She kept her job only for independence, so that she could do the work she was really called for: public service, change and upliftment of society.

The plan included her sister-in-law, my Aunt Rita, Uncle Percy's wife, who had flown over from their home in Trinidad to stay with Granny Mirri for a while. Aunt Rita had two sons, the toddler Reggie and the baby Algy, a newborn like me. She was apparently quite happy to look after me as well as her own children, leaving Mum free to work full-time.

'I couldn't imagine being in the kitchen with the pots and pans,' Mum told me later, and it became her standard reply as to why she'd always been that very rare being, a working mother of the early 50s.

But I refused the bottle. It simply wasn't good enough. It was the breast or nothing. My rebellion against the bottle proved a dilemma; it upset the plan. Fortunately, Mum was able to come back every day for lunch, as did most employees and schoolchildren who lived close enough to their schools and workplaces. Georgetown was a small city, its centre literally minutes away from our Lamaha Street house, and commuting for childcare was quick and easy. And so Mum brought me to Aunt Rita every morning when she went to work, returned for her (and my) lunch break, and picked me up after work. It was an ideal situation, for her, if not for me.

Aunt Rita must have had her hands full, but she was not alone as caregiver; Aunt Leila and to a lesser extent Granny Mirri – the women of the household – pitched in valiantly to keep that loudly protesting baby fed, consoled, reassured that she'd not been abandoned forever. Unfortunately, it didn't work very well.

I was a baby with very strong feelings about the situation, and very strong lungs, and unafraid of making the whole household aware of that fact. I defiantly and stridently refused the bottle to the very end. I demanded my mother and her breast. I demanded cuddles, and from her alone. And I demanded these things often and loudly. I screamed the place down; I kicked and wrestled with them all. I wanted her, only her. I must have driven those poor women frantic.

But somehow, we all survived. I presumably got used to the reality that Mum was absent for most of the day. I settled down. I became a quiet baby and toddler, too quiet, maybe. I managed to push those wounds of abandonment far away, and became that good and quiet child adults love to praise. Yet the wounds remained, deep inside. I know this because I felt them all my life, and later, much later, healing them became the leading motive of my life. They were wounds that would not pull me down, but instead urged me to find a cure; one that would delve deep enough to reach that place of soreness and, eventually, propel me forward. There was a void. I missed her, and even before I had the thoughts and words to know it, I had to learn to fill it.

I missed, most of all, the love that goes into a meal hand-prepared by a devoted mother. I have no memory of her ever cooking a meal for me, an act so completely integral to the nourishing role of a mother. Later, as a mother myself, I realised that that most precious, lasting bond of mother to newborn was never established between us. We had to build it, later, carefully and consciously; and we both paid a price. But that was to come later, much later.

Mum simply was not a maternal woman. She lacked the skills that go into responding to and caring for a little baby, into nourishing a tiny human being. Perhaps she should never have had a child, but she did not regret it for a moment, and lacking those skills did not make her a bad mother, just a different one. Her love for me was always there; it was the ability to express it that she lacked. I missed her, but just as the body miraculously learns to adapt and adjust itself to whatever circumstances it is faced with, and sometimes even strengthens itself under adverse conditions, so, too, I learned to adjust and grow despite those missing maternal elements.

A plant can grow strong and stable even in rough and stony ground. So, too, did I learn not only to survive, but to thrive.

But missing Mum at so early a stage led to a lifelong burning hunger in me for deep, abiding, stable love. I was constantly aware of a sense of a vacuum within me, an unfulfilled need for love and closeness. Later, this led to an inability and reluctance to show my own feelings, a fear of rejection, and an almost pathological shyness that would often be misinterpreted by others as lack of warmth or interest. It was actually quite the opposite. I wanted *more* closeness than others were able to give, and so I pre-emptively retreated from them, aware of the risk of rejection, unable to open up emotionally yet longing to do just that. And at the same time, it led to an almost preternatural independence and will to work everything out for myself, without referring to adults; a rejection, even, of outside assistance. An inner stoicism and determination to resolve all problems on my own.

As a mother, Mum might have been far from that perfect, tender image of motherhood. But no mother is perfect and, aware of this deficit, she did what loving, caring working mothers have always done: she found for me the very best care from women who could do all the things she couldn't, and do them well. Aunt Rita was the first, but not the only person to care for me in my early months. Aunt Leila was there as backup, and when Aunt Rita returned to Port-of-Spain, it was Aunt Leila who picked up the maternal slack in full. She became my ersatz mother, and it was she who nourished and guided me through those early pre-memory years in Lamaha Street.

Mum's own apparent lack of tenderness to me as a baby was deceptive. She doted on me, and even if she didn't have the ability – or the time – to show it, I certainly knew it. 'Marriage wasn't for me,' she often told me as I was growing up. 'But I don't regret being married for one second because your father gave me the most precious thing in my life: you.'

And she'd hug me and take me to nice places and read me stories. It certainly wasn't all work and no play. We were still a family, and she was trying hard to make it work.

Chapter Six

Long Leave

Mum might have rejected the traditional roles of motherhood, but she was there for me in other ways. My earliest years can be divided into two clear parts: pre-England, and post-England. I have no memory whatsoever of pre-England; I know only that we were a family of three, living in Mum's house in Subryanville, and that she brought me to Lamaha Street while she worked and collected me after work, and that Aunt Leila was my primary caretaker there. My precious time with Mummy was limited to her afternoons and weekends, a time she balanced with her voluntary activism.

I know, from hearsay and from photos, that it was a good, relaxed and healthy time. There are pictures of me on the beach, or in the gardens, of us together and apart; in an age when cameras were not an everyday possession, those photos tell me stories of happy times, a much-loved child, and devoted parents.

Mummy and Daddy would take me for walks along the beach, just over the Sea Wall across the road from our house, me clinging to their hands. They'd take me to the playground at the botanical gardens and help me slide down the slide and push me on the swings. We'd go to the zoo, where we'd stand at the manatee pond and whistle for its lumbering form to emerge out of the watery depths. We'd throw grass in the pond to feed it, and I'd giggle when it came up to eat. They were happy days; being together during Mummy's precious free time more than compensated for the agonies of her absences.

What I loved most of all was storytime, when Mummy made up for all the time we'd lost by reading to me. It was always the climax of the day. Those were the times I treasured the most: precious hours cuddled up to her at bedtime within the protective white tent of the mosquito net, she leaning against the backboard with an arm around me.

My favourite books as a young child were Noddy stories. But Mummy also wrote stories of her own. She'd type them out meticulously, and staple the pages together into a little booklet about mice and cats and birds and ocelots and turtles, then read them to me, and those were the stories I loved most of all.

But I also loved it when she read me poems, especially the stories and poems of A.A. Milne, which embedded themselves into my memory.

My very favourite was the poem 'The Dormouse and the Doctor', about the little dormouse who was so very content in a bed of red geraniums and blue delphiniums. So happy and carefree! But then one day he got sick, and the doctor came hurrying round and said that the best cure was yellow and white chrysanthemums. And so, without even a by-your-leave, they dug up the bed of blue delphiniums and red geraniums:

And they planted chrysanthemums (yellow and white).
'And now,' said the Doctor, 'we'll soon have you right.'

But they didn't. The little dormouse only grew sicker and sicker, and spent the rest of his life yearning and pining for geraniums (red) and delphiniums (blue). That poor little dormouse! In the end, all he could do was imagine he was back in his own bed, back in paradise.

She read this poem to me, over and over again, at my demand, just as I was learning words and language, and it has remained embedded in my mind. And other poems too: the one about the king who wanted a big red Indian rubber ball for Christmas, and the one about the boy who told his mother not to go down to the end of the road without consulting him, and the one about Emily, who could not be found for over a week.

Like small children everywhere, I insisted: 'Read it again!' Over and over again, she kindly complied. There's a running theme throughout all of these poems: a thread of loneliness, and a longing for things you can't have, whether it's a big red India rubber ball, or butter on your bread, or delphiniums blue and geraniums red. But there's also the recurring theme of losing your mother, and adjusting and growing strong even if everything goes wrong. I knew many of them by heart even before we went off to England, and I never forgot them, for they reflected a deeper and truthful part of my early childhood: that sense of something missing. I missed *her*.

But then came long leave, and London, and I had her all to myself for several months.

'Darling! We're going to go on a big ship! We're going across the ocean! You'll see snow! You'll see Piccadilly Circus!'

What is snow, I must have wondered. I knew what a circus was, and Piccadilly Circus sounded particularly exciting, and so did sailing off on a big ship, like the ones we'd see chugging out of the Demerara River and growing smaller as they headed out into the Atlantic, finally disappearing into the hazy horizon. We often went to watch the ships at the Groyne, and now I'd be sailing away on one myself. For a little girl of three, this was a huge adventure. But the best thing of all was that we were *all* going. All three of us. Mummy wouldn't be going to work for a while. I'd have her all to myself, all day long, every day.

Mummy and Daddy, as civil servants, were both entitled to long leave every three years, a holiday granted to British citizens who lived in all the corners of the far-flung Empire to enable them to return Home now and again for six months. If the sun never set on the British Empire, it still revolved around those tiny islands west of mainland Europe. It *was* the sun; the colonies revolved around it.

Most British subjects considered the British Isles Home. They'd return Home every few years to visit the families they left behind: the children they'd shunted off to boarding schools, their parents, brothers and sisters, nieces and nephews. They went Home to indulge in their deeply missed Sunday roasts and to shop again at Harrods. To walk in woodland paths or wallow in the nostalgia of a proper frosty Christmas. They came Home in tall ships from India, Malaya, Africa, Australia, China and the West Indies. They travelled through the Suez Canal, around the Cape of Good Hope and across the Atlantic.

Mummy and Daddy were also British subjects, but for them Home was right here, in British Guiana, and going off to England on long leave was a grand six-month holiday abroad. Great Britain did not discriminate between white home-grown British and brown British. We were simply British, and this was a well-deserved holiday.

My parents both took an advance on their salaries, and off we all went. I didn't know it then, but it was the last time we'd all be together, the three of us, as a family. Was this a last-ditch attempt to save the marriage? If so, it failed.

It was during this final family time that my first active memories seep into consciousness, and find permanence. Snippets of life that lodged themselves into my mind to stay there permanently, reminding me that this was my first awakening. The snow, the elephant, the fire. The catseyes, Tweety Bird and, most of all, the two stone lions and the anonymous hand leading me up a gently sloping staircase. They are fleeting things, evanescent and ethereal in their elusiveness, and yet I can't escape them. They are true memories, though I cannot vouch for their absolute truth.

A smile in the snow

Those months in England proved something of an idyllic holiday, a last grand time together before it all came crashing down. Mummy stayed behind in England to further her education. Daddy and I returned to BG. They were never to reunite.

Abandoned, seemingly, by both parents, I settled into a new life in Lamaha Street.

Mum, far across the ocean, in England, remained as a void. *Missing Mummy* abides as a lasting memory of that time, the overriding theme, even as I laughed and played with my animal and insect friends in the backyard, and discovered the world and pretended all was right. *Missing Mummy* was the underlying reality in everything I did, a vacuum never filled by distractions. She was the most important person in my life, and I had lost her.

Was I even capable, at three years old, of dealing with loss? That, of course, depended on the surrounding circumstances, as well as my own ability to cope with inner pain. Fortunately, those two elements were strong; I pieced together all the ingredients on which I thrived: Granny's lap, backyard adventures, and Daddy. But the overarching theme of these first post-England times was Aunt Leila, who stepped into the breach and took over my care. There couldn't have been a better aunt.

Chapter Seven

In Loco Parentis

Aunt Leila was the very image of a devout and taciturn spinster aunt, but she wasn't actually a spinster. Just like Mum, she was a rare creature of her era: a divorcée. Aunt Leila had once been married. I knew this because of her surname, and I'd always thought she'd been widowed, but this wasn't the case. When I cleared out my mother's papers, long after Aunt Leila's death, I finally understood. Her husband had cheated on her, dumped her for a younger woman and left her basically destitute. The divorce had not been pretty.

As an unmarried young woman without a job, Aunt Leila moved back in with her mother, Granny Mirri, and took on the role of housekeeper at Lamaha Street. All domestic chores fell to her. She cooked and cleaned, and looked after me, Mum and Granny and everyone else who lived there as well as anyone who came and went. She was the good spirit of the house.

Aunt Leila swept and mopped and polished the wooden floors of the drawing room and gallery in the traditional way: down on her hands and knees with a tin of Mansion Wax and a soft cloth, each floorboard given a thorough treatment lengthwise. She'd mix some turpentine into the Mansion to soften it and make it easier to apply. When each inch of the floor was thoroughly waxed, and the wax was dry, it had to be polished with a weighted buffer. When I was small, I'd get to stand on the buffer to add more weight; as I grew older, I added my own spice to the process by doing the twist over the floor with soft cloths tied around my feet. The floors would end up polished to a high shine, with the smell of floor polish pervading the house. The Lamaha Street house came into its full glory with that unique smell: the heady fragrance of glow and elbow grease and domestic pride.

The kitchen floor, although also wooden, went unpolished. Instead, Aunt Leila would once again get down on hands and knees and scrub it front to back, using a bucket of water, a worn-down bar of Ajax household soap, a metal scrubber and a rag for the final dry-off.

The kitchen floor was thus kept spotless, but the walls were another story. In the old days, most people used to cook with a wood-burning stove, which still stood, unused, at the back of the kitchen. The soot-pervaded smoke from it had turned the walls and ceiling completely black so we had a black-walled kitchen, but with a floor you could eat off.

Aunt Leila cooked on a two-burner kerosene stove. It had a fat bottle of kerosene upside down on one end, and two wick burners. You turned the wick up and adjusted the flame to blue to cook, and down to lower the flame or extinguish the fire. Aunt Leila managed to cook the most delicious meals on this contraption, or so I'm told, since I did not eat them, being the picky eater that I was. Back then, as a toddler – now thankfully weaned – I made do with porridge and fruit.

I took Aunt Leila's role for granted during my childhood. But later, as an adult, I became curious and asked Mum: 'What did we live on, you, me, Aunt Leila and Granny? Who supported that household?'

'I did,' she replied. Mum was the breadwinner for all of us, the 'husband' of the household, with Aunt Leila as the 'housewife'. Both traditional roles perhaps, but both filled by women.

Aunt Leila, *in loco parentis,* was scary. She was very strict, but fair. She was the one who laid down the rules, and she didn't much care for noisy children. Thank goodness I wasn't noisy at all, and

I had no one to create havoc with anyway. She provided well for me, ensured I was fed, watered and clothed, and did her best to instil in me the virtues of politeness and obedience. She took me for walks and visits to her friends. I looked up to her no end, but I would not eat her food. She was, I've been told, a wonderful cook, but I was a terrible eater.

I was a quiet, well-behaved child, but fussiness with food was an obstinacy no one was able to break: not my parents, not my grannies, not even strict, scary Aunt Leila. I wouldn't eat this and I wouldn't eat that. Once I had sorted out what I would and wouldn't eat, all I had for lunch, ever, was a single chicken drumstick. That became my midday meal, year in, year out.

Aunt Leila, strict as she was, left to herself would have probably trained this fussiness out of me, but she had to follow Mum's rules, and Mum said I had to make my own choices. I was not to be forced to eat anything. If all I wanted for lunch was a drumstick, all I should be given was a drumstick. It must have been frustrating for poor Aunt Leila. None of this 'You'll eat what's in front of you!' or 'You're not leaving the table until…', which I suspect would have been her natural response.

In retrospect, I think it was the sight and smell of raw meat in the markets that put me off a lot of food that was put in front of me, as most traditional meals were meat-based. I was an instinctive vegetarian from the start; I couldn't stand even the sight of red meat and blood. I made a concession with chicken because the carcasses were pale and showed little or no blood. I also managed fish and shrimp and crab. It was the *blood* I could not stomach. I was then, and still am now, most unadventurous when it comes to food. I can eat the same thing day after day and never get bored: ascetic by nature.

Aunt Leila accordingly placed on my plate, every day, a single drumstick and nothing else. These were Mum's orders. As a result, I've never even tasted all the apparently delicious dishes Guyana is known for, and these days, when Guyanese in the diaspora wax poetic about pepper-pot, or garlic pork, or *metemgee*, I only shrug. You can't miss what you've never had. Between meals, I also had a few culinary quirks; peanut butter from the jar was one of my favourite snacks, as well as powdered milk straight from the tin.

Then there was fruit. I might not have eaten regular meals, but I loved fruit. Who could resist those local fruits with their dripping juice, ambrosia from BG's lush green backyards, bounty brought in from the Pomeroon or Berbice or even from across the Lamaha Canal? We lived in a paradise of mouth-watering fruit. A ripe juicy mango, succulently orange, sliced on a plate and smelling of heaven; slabs of fresh pineapple lightly sprinkled with salt, or a glorious guava, or soursop, or sapodilla. Local apples: golden-apples, mammee apples, star apples and sugar apples. Tangerines and oranges and apple-bananas. Grapefruit, lovingly shredded by Granny Mirri. And all the juices and snacks derived from fruit: banana fritters, guava jelly, tamarind balls, sweet and savoury plantain chips, not to mention soursop and coconut and mango ice cream. Aunt Leila made some kind of fruit juice every day: sorrel, or pineapple; orange or grapefruit or tamarind. *Those* were the foods of the gods, as far as I was concerned.

And genips! We had two enormous genip trees in the Lamaha Street backyard, and when it was genip season we'd hire boys to swarm up into the upper branches and pick those bunches of swollen fruit. They were so unappetising in appearance, in their taut green leathery skins, but once you popped them open with your teeth, tearing those golden balls of flesh, and you plopped them into your mouth with the tart-sweet succulence sinking into your taste buds, then you had a foretaste of heaven. I've never known a fruit as addictive as genips. I could eat them forever, finish a whole bag, a whole bucket even.

I had a very sweet tooth. I also loved cake, and Aunt Leila was a magnificent baker. I don't believe we had a proper oven; I suppose she baked her cakes by placing the cake pan, raised, in large cooking pots. Her cakes were delicious, but most delicious of all were the batter ladles and the bowl itself, which was all mine to lick out. Being an only child certainly had its advantages.

All these ingredients came from the market. Every morning, Aunt Leila went shopping for the day's supply, and if I was at home and did not have school, or on Saturdays, she'd take me with her. Georgetown had two markets, Bourda and Stabroek, the latter being the nearest to our home. We had no car; the only person in the Lamaha Street community who had one was Uncle Archie. He owned a white Austin, but he never took anyone anywhere. And so we walked, there and back. A parasol held over our heads, a basket looped over her arm, we'd stroll off together. 'Hook me, my dear!' she'd say as we crossed the road to the Lamaha Street pavement.

'Hook me, my dear!' became one of my most potent memories of her, looking down at me, poking out her elbow for me to reach up whenever we came to a crossing and had to wait for the traffic to pass. When our arms weren't linked, I'd skip along beside her beneath the flamboyant red-blossomed trees on the Waterloo Street central walkway. We'd take a shortcut through the Promenade Gardens, which were just around the corner. I'd cling to her skirts or her arm as we wandered through the stalls of Stabroek Market, afraid of getting lost in the melee, while she chose the fruit and vegetables and meat needed that day. She'd argue with market-women about the price of fish, crab or chicken, or stop to have a chat with this acquaintance or that friend she'd run into. Sometimes she'd buy me a little treat: a peanut brittle, an I-cee soda, or even a Popsicle or a Fudgicle.

Georgetown was a miniature paradise. It had a character of its own: mellow, slow-paced, overflowing with greenery and flowers; white wooden houses on stilts, nestled in lush gardens; wide avenues with central walkways shaded by flamboyants. I missed Mum, but now less desperately so, for I lived in this little corner of heaven. I had the backyard and the animals and the ants. I had a home, and Lamaha Street for the next few years became the centre of my universe, with or without Mummy and Daddy, separate or apart. I had to cope. There was no choice. I had to claim my home, and my place in it, small as I was.

Chapter Eight

A Houseful of Adults

I lived in a ménage of adults, with me underfoot between them all, running in and out of the house. Lamaha Street became my home from the time I was three, newly returned from England, to the time I returned there for boarding school, aged ten. It was a household of adults, or rather a houseful of women; at first three single women: a spinster, a divorcée, a widow. Later, it was four women, when Mum joined the gang, making it two divorcées. The spinster was a lovely little lady I called Aunt Edna, a Bible-study friend of Aunt Leila, a single working woman of advanced age, and not a real aunt.

Like Uncle Archie, Aunt Edna was a paying guest, but unlike him, she was very much a family member and a person who loved company, mine especially.

I loved visiting Aunt Edna. She lived in the annex, the nicest bedroom of all. You accessed the annex across a sort of bridge above the stairs. It had windows on three sides and it was large and light and airy. Aunt Edna was friendly and warm, and had a secretarial job somewhere in town. Her hobby was crocheting. She crocheted countless doilies for the Blind Society, and spent her evenings after work sitting in the gallery with the rest of the family and any guests who might pop in, chatting away with everyone, briskly crocheting.

Evenings were a gathering-time for all the adults. Tall, thin, gregarious Aunt Effie from the back cottage would come, and so would the Van Sertimas from around the corner. Sometimes Aunt

Elma, Mum's second sister, came around as well, and Aunt Leila's former sister-in-law Aunty Dolly (it seems Aunt Leila's in-laws sided with her after the ugly divorce). All these ladies – and it was inevitably mostly women, with an occasional husband or two sprinkled in – would sit in the gallery for the evening, exchanging the day's news and gossiping. Such gatherings took place all over Georgetown; people visited each other, sat on comfortable chairs in countless galleries and verandas, discussing events of the gone day in a most congenial manner, sipping cool drinks occasionally laced with rum. That's what people do when there's no television, no on-call entertainment: they entertain each other, in person. They reach out to each other, and gather in each other's homes. Sometimes, I would join them, sitting in Granny's lap until I fell asleep, when Aunt Leila would carry me upstairs and lay me down in bed.

Apart from Aunt Edna's room there were three other interconnected bedrooms upstairs: mine, Aunt Leila's and Granny's; plus, a large upstairs shower room and a separate toilet, shared by all five adults and me. My bedroom was a large breezy corner room, the middle one, with two Demerara windows at the front and two sash windows at the side. I slept in a double bed in the centre of the room. A mosquito net hung above it, curled and knotted into itself during the day and tucked in around the mattress at night to form a ghostly white tent. Next to the bed there was a wardrobe, and on the window side a wash-hand stand with a ceramic jug of water, slightly cracked and patterned with flowers, and a matching basin. Everything was simple, furnished with practical pieces flung together willy-nilly. Nobody wasted a thought on aesthetics.

Above the wash-hand stand in my room hung a large portrait of a blond, long-haired Jesus, one hand held out invitingly, the other held on his heart: the very same portrait you'll find in a lot of Irish homes to this day. In a corner of the room, beneath one of the Demerara windows, stood the little blue desk where, later, I did my homework and wrote my stories.

As for Uncle Archie, Mum's first cousin, I didn't count him as part of the household because he wasn't. He slept at Lamaha Street, presumably used the bathroom and toilet, but otherwise came and went without talking to anyone. I don't believe he even ate there. He had a girlfriend somewhere, and a job. He came and went and between the girlfriend, his job, and his rifle practice, he had no time or inclination to mix with us females.

I was rather terrified of him because of his guns. Nevertheless, I would, now and again, sneak into his room – which was always left unlocked – to inspect them. There were so many of them, some on the wall, some in a bottom drawer, some in a box under the bed. I'd open the drawer and stare at them. I never touched them. They were probably not loaded, but guns were scary things, cowboy things, soldier things. They were fascinating but terrifying; you could kill people with guns. I wondered if Uncle Archie wanted to kill people; he was unfriendly enough to do so, was my reasoning. I kept away from him.

Our backyard at Lamaha Street, a huge area spreading out behind the house right up to a rickety paling at the back, its white paint peeling, was paradise encapsulated. Beyond the palings was a gutter, and another gutter ran along the front of the house. This was the case in most streets: gutters edged them, crossed by bridges leading to the houses. All of Georgetown was criss-crossed by gutters; they were the drainage channels, not only for household wastewater, but for the torrential rain that arrived like clockwork twice a year.

Roses grew in the front garden, but also a tangle of tall, leafy plants reaching up beside the front staircase. Along the stems and leaves of that plant crawled caterpillars, lugging along their bulky cocoons. I loved nothing more than to sit on the stairs and watch the green caterpillars hauling along their huge homes, and if I were lucky, I'd occasionally catch a glimpse of the emerging butterflies, colourful beings that flitted among the flowers of the front garden.

Behind the house stood the vat, a huge wooden barrel once used to collect rainwater. Before we had indoor plumbing, those barrels were Georgetown's source of water. In 1885 the city council installed water pipes throughout the town, and now the vat was used only for washing clothes. A washerwoman came once a week; she'd squat on a low stool next to the vat with her buckets, scrubbing board and worn-away cake of yellow household soap and scrub away. Lines of washing stretched across the backyard, sheets and undies flapping in the breeze, or, in the rainy season, under the house.

Behind the house stood a tiny cottage on short, stumpy stone pillars. Here lived another of Mum's cousins, Uncle Archie's sister Aunt Effie, and her husband, Uncle Beryl. They had no children, but now and then their niece, Jocelyn, came to visit them. Jocelyn was my age and we played together occasionally, but she lived far away, in Berbice, so our contact was limited. Jocelyn impressed me no end one day by pronouncing, with some authority, that 'air has weight'. I hardly believed her, but I took note. That pronouncement became my main childhood memory of Jocelyn, who is now a well-known Georgetown businesswoman and political activist.

Chapter Nine

The View from the Morris Chair

The gallery window functioned as Granny's sole entertainment and access to the world outside. There was a lot to see out there, on Lamaha Street, the longest east-to-west street in the city.

It was a busy street and the city's most northerly main road, running parallel to the Atlantic coast, forming a major vein between town and country. Much of the traffic coming down from the East Coast Demerara into central Georgetown passed our house. The traffic was mostly bicycles and dray carts: small ones pulled by donkeys, long ones pulled by bony horses. Schoolchildren rode past on bikes; Queen's College was just around the corner to the north, Bishops' High School around another corner to the south, and my own primary school, St Margaret's, around yet another corner, to the east.

At the Camp Street junction, just three houses down from our house, a tall thin policeman (all policemen were tall and thin to me!) in a dark blue uniform stood in the middle of the road, directing traffic. Bicycles would gather at each side of the junction, bunching up together, surrounding the cars and the carts, and swarm forward when the policeman beckoned them on, south into the town centre, east or west along Lamaha Street, or north towards the Sea Wall.

Across the street from our house, on the far, north side, there were no houses, just the Lamaha Canal, parallel to the street. Georgetown being a coastal city six feet below sea level, with two rainy seasons in which water cascades down from above, it's not surprising that one of the major problems that it has faced throughout its history is water management. In the nineteenth century, the availability of water for domestic use was a major issue. Neither seawater nor rainwater floods could solve that problem.

Thus, the Lamaha Canal came into being. The canal runs the full length of Lamaha Street, parallel to the Sea Wall. It was completed in 1829 through the labour of hundreds of slaves. In those early days, all along the canal trenches branched off to supply the city's residents with water. Then, in 1885, a modern system of pipes was installed, delivering water into Georgetown's homes. The north–south canals were filled in, and became the foundations for the beautiful tree-lined avenues that eventually gave Georgetown the reputation of Garden City of the Caribbean.

Day after day, Granny would sit in her Morris chair at the window, gazing out at the street and the canal beyond it to the patches of land where East Indian farmers managed their allotments, toiling all day in the hot sun. Beyond the allotments was a clear view of fields, as well as the distant tree-shaded district of Eve Leary, dedicated to police matters: administrative buildings and barracks in cream-painted wood, shaded by coconut palms. And beyond them, the Sea Wall.

Aunt Leila and I, hand in hand, would walk up to the Sea Wall most afternoons and every Sunday, first crossing Lamaha Street to the pavement on the other side. We'd turn north up Camp Road, towards the Sea Wall. There, to the left, stood the Eve Leary Mounted Police Headquarters with a stable full of horses; beautiful, well-groomed, well-trained horses, who pranced and clattered through the streets, in direct contrast to the skinny nags that pulled the dray carts.

Further down Camp Road was a street leading west towards the police barracks, the parade ground, and the sedate residential district known as Kingston. To the right stood the low cream buildings of Queen's College, the prestigious secondary school for boys, the school Dad and his brothers had attended as well as the rival political leaders Forbes Burnham and Cheddi Jagan. British politician Trevor Phillips is another graduate, as was E.R. Braithwaite, author of *To Sir, With Love*.

The Sea Wall was the centre of the community on weekdays and Saturday afternoons once the heat of the sun had relented, but it was especially so on Sundays. That was the day when Georgetowners of all walks of life, all colours, all races, all social strata, went out to take in the bracing salty breeze. Everyone dressed in their Sunday best, the men in dapper suits and ties, the women in the latest fashions, their hair tucked primly into their lacy hats, girls all in their finest frills and boys as smart as smart can be. We all headed for the Promenade, the widened area of the Sea Wall, straight north as the crow flies from our house. That was where we all walked with our families, or sat on one of the benches, and listened to the police brass band in the bandstand playing rousing melodies that conjured up the glory and the power of Empire. Aunt Leila would dress me in frothy dresses with sticky-out skirts, shiny shoes and frilly socks, and ribbons in my plaits. Aunt Leila would meet friends and chat with them, and I'd meet other children and we'd play hopscotch or skipping-rope games, all underscored by music of that big brass band.

If the tide was out you could walk down to the beach, and children would play in the sand and watch the crabs scurrying back and forth from their holes. Or you could walk along the narrow stone jetties jutting out into the Atlantic, or stroll westward along the wall until you came to the Groyne, the wide embankment where the Demerara River met the Atlantic Ocean. You could stand on the Groyne, wind-whipped, and watch ships coming in and leaving, big ships, sometimes ocean liners, bound for the docks further inland.

The canals, the gutters, the ocean, the rain. Water reigned in BG. The very word Guiana means Land of Many Waters, and we certainly knew it. But of all these sources of water, there was nothing like rain to make a little girl know that water was the very essence of life on earth, to make her feel her own very essence as fluid, soft, a flowing stream of impressions and feelings, spirit searching for expression. Nothing called to spirit as much as rain.

Rain! It came as a deluge from above and settled as a flood below. In the rainy season much of Georgetown stood knee-deep under water for weeks, but the Dutch had built our homes well and we were always high and dry in our houses on stilts. Rain rattled and pounded on our corrugated-iron roof, and as there was no ceiling between the roof and my bed, I'd lie there wrapped up warmly in sheets and blankets and, huddled under the mosquito-net tent, listen to the roar of water as it drummed the roof. The rainfall was so heavy, it sounded like an ocean pouring down upon the iron roof, thundering overhead. During a storm, flashes of lightning would light up the whole room, and then I'd hold my breath, counting the seconds in anticipation of the ear-splitting crash of thunder, so loud it was as if a bomb had exploded in the night sky, tearing the world apart.

But there I was, safe and sound, wrapped up in my sheet, snuggled under the mosquito-net tent, all warm and cosy, hugging a pillow. Nothing in the world gave as much of a sense of deep contentment.

Outside, the water fell in solid sheets and rose and rose. Soon all the houses and trees and telegraph poles stood in a solid lake, and cars crept through the water, drivers unable to see where the roads ended and the side gutters and trenches began. For us children, once the sun came out from behind its blanket of clouds, this was the time to put on our bathing suits and start our real adventure. I'd dash down the stairs to play in the flooded yard. I made rafts and played boat with friends, waded through the knee-high water, imagined myself stranded on a desert island. We'd use the rafts to attempt to sail the ocean at our doorstep. We'd sit ourselves in blown-up car inner tyres and yank each other through the water, oblivious to the warnings of our elders: 'Don' fall in the trench!' and, of course, the usual 'You-all gon' get ringworm!' Somehow, we all survived, all the better for the memories. We bellowed out the 'Song of Guyana's Children': *Onward, upward, may we ever go, day by day in strength and beauty grow, till at length we each of us may show, what Guyana's sons and daughters can be.* The words nested within us and seeds sprouted until it all became true.

Chapter Ten

A Houseful of Children

Back home from England, Daddy returned to the family that was *his* nest: that vibrant, somewhat chaotic house on Crown Street where his mother Winnie and her husband George and just about everyone else lived. The one-storeyed Crown Street house was half the size of the Lamaha Street one, but with twice the number of inhabitants. And just as Granny Mirri's house was full of adults, Granny Winnie's was full of children, and always had been.

Like the Lamaha Street house, it was a typical wooden house, built on stilts, with three bedrooms, plus a boarded-off section of the gallery occupied by Uncle Denis. Somehow, everybody fitted in. Three adults and five children lived there, not to mention visitors popping in and out.

Daddy came often to pick me up in his green Ford Prefect and bring me to his family, and I was as much at home in Crown Street as I was in Lamaha Street. The house stood in Queenstown, a quiet, residential area to the east of town, with a corner shop down the road where you could buy sweet drinks and peanut brittle and put coins into a bubblegum machine that gave you big round multicoloured balls of sticky gum. There was a Catholic primary school, the Good Shepherd, just around the corner, and around another corner, a children's playground. Down the road were the cricket club grounds. When a major match was on there'd be mayhem; boys and young men swarming up the trees surrounding the high fences to watch the matches for free, yelling encouragements at their home team and favourite players. Daddy and all his brothers were keen cricketers, and as boys had no doubt sat in the branches of those trees.

Granny Winnie had raised eight sons. Most of them married and had children: me and my cousins, with more grandchildren being born every year well into the 50s and 60s. At this point, in the early 50s, almost all of us still lived in the colony, and that Crown Street house was the Westmaas family hub. But there was a tragic reason why five children lived there.

Long before I was born, tragedy struck; my Uncle Rupert's wife died, leaving their five children, two girls and three boys, without a mother, the youngest but a baby. Granny Winnie, her husband Pa and Uncle Denis, the only unmarried son, filled that void, raising those five half-orphans as best they could. And so now, the house at Crown Street swarmed with children: upstairs and downstairs, climbing trees in the yard, roller-skating on the pavement outside and galivanting through the quiet neighbourhood. The Westmaas children were everywhere, and I was one of them, motherless too for the time being, a shy little three-year-old desperate to find her own place in the world.

However, I was much smaller than Uncle Rupert's children, a few of whom were already in their teens. I looked up to them, took my cues from them, followed their example. I knew that they, too, were motherless, even more so than me. They too lived with their granny, and not with their parents. I understood that families come in all sorts of shapes, and my big cousins became leading lights for me. They were all so knowledgeable, so clever, so mature! If they could do it, so could I. Of course, being only three, I did not actually *think* this. But in retrospect, my big Crown Street cousins were major influences during this time of separation, this time of great turbulence, of sorting out my place in the big wide world.

Where was home? Was home here, where I was but the smallest one of a horde, but with a loving father who always had time to take me on his lap and read me a Noddy story? Or was it in Lamaha Street, with all the space in the world, exploring, all on my own, the nooks and crannies, trees and bushes of what seemed a vast backyard – but motherless? Neither Aunt Leila nor Granny replaced Mum. I missed her dreadfully. I wanted that family. I wanted that home. I wanted it all. But it was not to be. As Aunt Leila repeated constantly: *'I want' never gets*. I learned quite early that life doesn't necessarily deliver the things you desperately want but that you have to cope nevertheless, and not only cope, but thrive. In the end, that's what I did.

One of the greatest attractions at Granny Winnie's home was Uncle Denis, our favourite uncle. Uncle Denis was a clown and a curiosity. He was the one brother who never married or had a family, but he didn't need children because he had all of us, his nieces and nephews. We would eventually grow into a horde of at least twenty, from the smallest baby up to the eldest, Ron, who was already almost an adult. Brilliant and wayward and often a thorn in the sides of his brothers, Uncle Denis himself stayed childlike all his life.

For us he was the absolute hero. No one else had an uncle who could wiggle his ears, and had such a never-ending flow of jokes and funny anecdotes at his disposal. No one else had an uncle who would lie on the floor and blow up his tummy into a trampoline for tiny feet. He could push a needle through his cheek and retrieve it from his mouth. He could make his thumb, and other objects, mysteriously disappear behind his ear. Uncle Denis made children laugh – but he made them study, as well.

The only job Uncle Denis ever had was as private after-school teacher in just about every subject, for he knew everything, and what he didn't know he taught himself, including foreign languages such as German. Scores of students passed through his hands and he'd tutor them in every subject: French, Latin or arithmetic, Uncle Denis was there to help. He never took a penny for those lessons, and all his life remained dependent on his parents or his brothers.

But it worked, because material objects were of no importance to Denis. He'd give away items of clothing, money and food to anyone who asked him. Many asked even when they had no need, but he didn't care: he simply gave.

Denis was a devout Christian, so much so that he once decided to follow in Christ's footsteps by fasting for forty days and forty nights. I don't think he made it to the end, but his devotion was a bit of a thorn in my father's side, for Dad was the opposite: a devoted atheist. Most Sunday mornings would see Uncle Denis and my dad at Dad's house, arguing about Christian theology until my stepmother Faye called out, 'Lunch!'

Uncle Denis became an icon of Georgetown, remembered fondly by many. He usually wore khaki knee-length shorts and long socks with a short-sleeved shirt, its pocket stuffed with pens contained in a pocket protector advertising some business or other. He liked to be out and about, roaming the streets of Georgetown on his rusty old bicycle. If ever he saw you on the street, he'd stop you with a shout and wave, leap off his bicycle and come up grinning, tell you a joke, guffawing at it himself, and ride off again. It was most embarrassing if you were with a friend.

But now, in those Mummy-starved months after my return from England, Uncle Denis became one of the main anchors in my life. It would have been easy for me to get lost among all the cousins, but Uncle Denis gave his attention to each child equally, and kept me giggling and entertained so that I was not once eclipsed by the sheer number of children at Granny Winnie's house.

However, beneath it all, beneath the fun and games, the animals and insects at Lamaha Street and the children and Daddy and Uncle Denis at Crown Street, one thing remained: that void, that longing, that yearning for Mummy. When would she return? Would she ever come back? The months seemed like years, stretching into a never-ending eternity. And then, one day, she was back. And life would never be the same again.

Chapter Eleven

Dear John

Dad was a dedicated family man and father, but Mum was the wrong wife. While he imagined an idyllic family life where he could be the ideal hands-on father, Mum had very different ideas. She said no. Very firmly.

'I have to work!' she'd told Dad, and had been telling him from the very start. 'I can't be stuck at home!'

Dad probably thought that once the baby was there, she'd change. That she couldn't resist the maternal instinct, which would kick in once she held me in her arms, and all would be well. It didn't, and it wasn't. He found this out the hard way, having brought me all the way from England on a ship, and now acting as my sole guardian even though I lived elsewhere.

Then, at long last, she was back. Daddy took me to the dock to meet her. There she stood at the railing, waving at us! There she was, walking down the gangplank, carrying a small valise! And there she was, on firm ground! I sat on Daddy's shoulders as he pushed me through the milling crowd. Then he put me down and I rushed into her arms. She bent to put her valise down, then swept me into her arms, clung to me, told me how much she missed me, and it felt like the world was whole again. Only it wasn't.

'When will we go home, Mummy?' I asked, later, once Daddy had dropped us off at Granny's. But she shook her head.

'We aren't, darling. We'll be staying here, with Granny and Aunt Leila.'

'But… Daddy… home…'

Her eyes were sad. 'Sweetheart, I'm sorry.'

It was all too much to understand. I didn't know the word divorce. It was a new thing, a strange thing, unheard of really, even among the adults. Under the laws of the land at the time, adultery was the only legal ground for divorce, as was the case with Aunt Leila's separation. In Mum and Dad's case, however, there was no adultery involved. As far as I know, there was never any scandal attached to it. Somehow, Mum managed to get a 'clean' divorce.

And so, to my great disappointment, after Mummy's return from England we did not move back home, to that lovely breeze-filled house in Subryanville. The marriage was over. Daddy had never agreed with her decision to be a working mother with such a young child. It had been an ongoing point of contention, and that, for her, was reason enough to divorce him. She made her decision known in writing.

Much later, she showed me a copy of her typed Dear John letter. It read something like this:

> *Dear David, I would like a divorce. I am going to retain full custody of Sharon but you can see her as often as you want. Sincerely, Eileen*

That was Mum all over. Crisp, neat, no wasted words, no sentimentality, no self-pity, no complaining, no mess. Instead, there was kindness and fairness, even as she dealt my father a devastating blow.

And so it was that Mum, on her return from England, moved in with Granny Mirri and Aunt Leila and me. Dad went back to stay with his mother in the crowded Crown Street house. She rented out the Subryanville house. It was all over. A new beginning, and my little life once again turned topsy-turvy.

Mum had brought two special things back from England: a certified qualification as a Palantypist, and a Palantype machine. In both cases, she was the first in the colony. The Palantype machine was a state-of-the-art device, very cutting-edge. It resembled a tiny typewriter, with only twenty-nine keys in all, on a tilted keyboard. It looked almost like a toy, a compact little thing that used special paper – a roll about two inches wide, which rotated through the machine as she typed, emerging sprinkled with mysterious symbols vertically spaced out down the paper. Its function was to record speech in mechanical shorthand, and it operated at the rate of regular speech. The fastest such system known, it was very advanced for the time. It was the only device of its kind in the country, and Mum the only certified Palantypist. *That* was the reason she'd stayed behind in England.

With her new qualifications, Mum soon found employment as a Hansard reporter, sitting in parliament and recording all the debates. Her workplace was in the mahogany-panelled parliament chamber in the Public Buildings, a rare example of nineteenth-century Renaissance architecture in Georgetown. Her office was right next door to the chamber, opening on to the long balcony that led from it right across the building to the prime minister's office.

In later years, when I would visit her at work, I ran into Prime Minister Forbes Burnham more than once, strutting along with his entourage, but, shy as I was, I scuttled out of his way. Burnham was to me a formidable man, unlike the opposition leader Cheddi Jagan, my father's boss, who was affable and child-friendly.

Symbolic of my childhood life in general, I yoyoed back and forth between the governing parent, Mum, and the opposition, Dad, when all I wanted was one happy family with peace and love between us all. Long before divorce became almost the norm, I was an innocent victim of a broken marriage. I did not like it at all, and blamed Mum.

Why had she done this to me, to us? Now, at three years of age, I was too young to comprehend the reasons and explanations. How could I understand the dynamics of a mismatched marriage, the feelings of a mother who needed to be financially independent? What did I know of women's rights, and her desire to work outside the home, of her refusal to stay in the kitchen with all the pots and pans? What other conclusion could I come to but that I wasn't enough for her, that I bored her?

As I grew older, I especially resented the fact that I was the only child in our entire circle of friends and relations who lived in a broken family. And, since I knew the reason for the break-up – Mum, candid as ever, had explained that it was because they couldn't agree on whether she should look after me at home or not – I also knew that I was to blame. I had split them apart. They had been perfectly happy before my arrival, before I produced needs they couldn't fulfil as a couple. I understood. It was all my fault.

All my cousins lived in proper families: both the offspring of Mum's siblings and those of Dad's brothers. Mum's sister Elma was married to Uncle Frank and had two children, Mirri and Mervyn, younger than me. They lived together with their mum and dad, and came to visit us in Lamaha Street, and then went home again, where their mummy cooked nice meals for them, and if you went to their house there'd be cake and snacks and games to play. Whenever there was a birthday party, Uncle Frank would play the piano for musical chairs and all of us would be racing around the chairs, trying to snag one. We'd play pussy in the corner and Simple Simon and pin the tail on the donkey. We'd sing and dance and it was all such fun, and the mummy would bring out a lovely home-baked birthday cake with candles, and when it was all over, all the other children would go home to their own mummies and daddies. Mirri and Mervyn had that. Why didn't I?

*

As for Dad's many brothers, Uncle Patrick was married to Aunt
Zena and they had two children, Gillian and Roderick, later to be
joined by Huw. They all lived together. Aunt Zena was an excellent
cook and there were always big meals round the table at their home.
Even though I didn't eat much, I always coveted a mummy like
that, one who cooked big tasty meals, with people sitting around
the table exclaiming how delicious everything was. At Lamaha
Street, Aunt Leila did all the cooking, all the cake-baking. But *my*
mummy never cooked.

Uncle Leonard was married to Aunt Trixie and they had three
children, Susan, Nancy and Mark. We all called Uncle Leonard
Uncle Bill, a nickname given by Uncle Denis because, it seemed,
Uncle Bill was short. It's an oblique reference to Bill Stumps in
Charles Dickens's *The Pickwick Papers*, and the word 'stumpy'.
Uncle Bill and Aunt Trixie lived in the county of Berbice, east of
Demerara, where he was office manager at Albion Estate, one of
the major sugar plantations that lined the coast.

I once spent a holiday with them, and that stay at Albion counts
among the most utterly glorious holidays of my childhood. I don't
remember the details so much, more the *feeling* I had when I was
there at Albion: a solid memory of sea breeze and sunshine, pristine
white, one-storey wooden houses on stilts, spaciously and sym-
metrically laid out on wide green lawns, a swimming pool, a tennis
court, and lots and lots of children. But mostly, the feeling of life
in a proper family, with a mummy at home who cooked and cared.

I too wanted a mummy and daddy at home, living with me, just
like all my cousins and all my friends. A Proper Family. I wanted a
mummy who was a Mrs, not a Miss. Later on, friends asked me if
I was a bastard, because my mummy called herself Miss Cox. She
had taken back her maiden name and the title Miss, just as if she'd
never been married, while I kept my father's surname. It was so

embarrassing having to tell them no, she's 'only' divorced. None of my friends had a divorced mother, and worse yet, one who called herself Miss Maiden-Name. Everybody else had a Proper Family. I was the only one without. I was an outsider, different. And it stung.

But feeling sorry for myself was not an option, and nor was moping around at home or throwing tantrums. This was life; I had to move on, and the next move was a big one: it was time for me to start school. Once again, everything changed.

Chapter Twelve

The Three Bears

Mrs Hunter bent down low, and gave me a huge smile.

'Well, hello! Are you the little bear? Here's a tiny chair, just for you!'

She gestured towards a small green chair. 'And look, here's a big chair for Daddy Bear, and a medium-sized chair for Mummy Bear!'

We all took our seats, and the meeting progressed, but from that first Three Bears moment on, I was in love with Mrs Hunter.

I didn't know it then, but Mrs Hunter was decades before her time, just like Mum. Her story, like Mum's, is worth telling, for it shows how a woman with the confidence of her own calling can rise above the ordinary and bring colour, innovation and change to the world she lives in. It was such rule-breakers who helped form and mould me and give me the confidence to listen for and discover my own true calling. Who helped mould my country in the 50s and 60s.

Mrs Hunter was a local woman of English heritage who many years previously had started a school of her own based on Montessori methods. Her little school had earned a reputation as the best primary school in Georgetown, yet it had had a less than encouraging start. Many parents, especially the 'home-grown' ones, were at first sceptical of Mrs Hunter's new-fangled teaching methods.

What was this new thing, learning through play and music? Learning is supposed to be a chore, after all, where children sit attentively in tidy rows, slate and slate-pencil in hand, doing what Teacher orders, or else – licks. 'Licks' – with a hand or a belt or even a ruler, on the hand or the backside – were the accepted methods of discipline in schools. Mrs Hunter's – Winifred's – school was different, because Winifred was different. There were no licks at Winifred's school.

Winnie, as she fondly became known, was raised in British Guiana in a house filled with music and books. Her mother taught her to read before she went to school and, during her early school days, her father responded to her eager questioning by guiding her to books and materials that would satisfy her curious nature.

It was the Latin mistress at St Rose's High School in Georgetown who unwittingly helped her to find her true calling.

It so happened that while in the sixth form, she decided to drop out of Latin classes. To keep her occupied during those sessions, the Latin teacher sent her to the infant school to help in the recently established Montessori classes. There, she found four- and five-year-olds sitting on the floor, arranging materials of various shapes, sizes and colours, tracing sandpaper letters and figures with their fingers, not a slate in sight. That was it for young Winnie. She spent many happy hours on the floor watching these little ones at work, and the spark that must have been smouldering all the time was kindled.

After completing the Senior Cambridge Overseas Exams, she went off to Edinburgh, where she trained as a nursery school teacher in the Froebel method. Montessori training was not available at the time, but this approach still glowed within her.

On returning home to British Guiana there came the excitement of opening a kindergarten of her own, made possible through the generosity of her parents, who not only helped her financially so she could buy furnishings and equipment but also provided the space, on the ground floor of their home. And she was off. St Margaret's School in Georgetown opened in January 1935, with seven girls and boys as pupils. It was mostly English parents, more accustomed to private schooling and more prepared to pay for schooling, who sent their children there.

At the start, increase in numbers was slow. 'Why pay for play?' parents thought. If there were free public schools run according to the established ways, why spend money on education? What was the point of this new-fangled agenda?

Parents were also wary about these new teaching methods. The children were not fixed to their seats, slates in hand, eyes on the teacher; parents thought they could not possibly be learning. Yet over the next seven years numbers continued to grow as parents converted to this new idea. In 1943, however, the school had to close because Winnie got married and moved away from Georgetown. Eight years and three children of her own later, the family moved back to Georgetown and the couple built a house at the back of the property belonging to Winnie's parents.

Following the birth of a son in 1954, and at the request of several parents, St Margaret's reopened with twenty pupils. I was among that very first new intake. The school was in Camp Street, a few blocks away from Lamaha Street, and it became a new haven and focal point for me, the launching pad of my life-to-be.

And so my first school was a Montessori school, at a time when the Montessori method was still an innovation of the future, a dream of progressive parents, and this in a country labelled by many others as 'backward'.

Those were happy days. I entered a world where we children sang songs, painted pictures and danced our way through school, all the while managing to read and write, to add and subtract, and to spell correctly. Most importantly, I was encouraged to think. I thrived, and loved school, and Mrs Hunter.

Above all, I discovered books. Once I learned to read myself, instead of having to be read to, I was flying. I'd always loved stories and had always had them read to me, but reading myself – that was heaven. An English writer named Enid Blyton had already started opening doors with her Noddy books, read to me at my insistence by Mummy and Daddy. But now that I could read on my own, new journeys and new worlds opened up before me.

The Magic Faraway Tree and *The Wishing Chair* sent me into magical realms far away from reality, worlds where everything was possible, where a spell could give you wings, where boring boundaries and tedious rules did not exist. I was right there with those intrepid children, climbing that magical tree and entering a land of sheer fantasy at the top, and meeting the most wonderful people: Dame Washalot, the Saucepan Man, Moon-Face, and countless others. I joined them in their adventures in the magical kingdoms in the treetops, lands that whooshed up and away and sometimes took you with them. They were all real to me.

As I grew older, *The Naughtiest Girl in the School* gave me new ideas: school, as well as being a place of learning, was a place of adventure. I soon progressed to St Clare's and Malory Towers, all of which put the notion into my head that boarding school in England was the place to be. A seed was planted in my little mind. It began to sprout.

At the same time, the Famous Five, the Secret Seven, the Adventure books, the Five Find-Outers: what incredible adventures were to be had if you just poked your nose into a book! Older cousins informed me later that that was where I was to be found from that time on: curled up somewhere, stuck in a book.

But my favourite place to curl up in was still Granny Mirri's lap, next to the window. There I felt safe and warm, even as my mind took flight, even as I joined the Famous Five on their boat to Kirrin Island, hunting down thieves or seeking buried treasure. There I knew the security of Granny's soft enfolding body, even as I climbed the Faraway Tree with my fictional friends and stepped into the magical lands swirling off from its topmost branches. There I could grow wings, take flight from a world that wasn't always to my liking.

One thing stood out in all the books I read. The children in these books lived in faraway lands unfamiliar to me: England, or Scotland, or America. Their backyards and gardens looked so different to my own; their towns and villages and cities were so different to the ones I knew. But most of all, they looked so different to *me*. These children were all white. They had blue eyes and soft straight hair that flopped over their foreheads or down their backs. And I felt instinctively that, because people like me were absent from these books, we simply didn't count. We were of lesser worth, not even worthy enough to be allowed into their books.

I felt that absence acutely. One particular episode that gnawed on me was in a Famous Five book. Anne, the youngest of the Five, was in her bedroom upstairs asleep, but woke to see a man's face in the window, peering in. She screamed, of course, and her big brother Julian came running. 'Oh, Julian!' sobbed Anne, 'what if it was a *black* man!'

That stung – the knowledge that even the children in the books I read knew that their race was the better one.

I already knew that white people ruled the world. After all, the Queen was white, and wasn't she at the top of the known world? Didn't we stand up to her in respect every time we went to the cinema? Wasn't our national anthem 'God Save the Queen'? And wasn't our governor-general white, and wasn't he at the head of us all in British Guiana? Wasn't everybody who was anything white-skinned?

That surely meant that to them, we people of colour were of inferior stock. Of lesser quality, and lower value. They must have thought we were subordinate. Not even worthy of being represented in the pages of a book! Not a single child in a story was brown like me. How could that be right?

It was a feeling that gnawed at me from inside. It just wasn't right. It just couldn't be true. Another, deeper feeling rose up in me: rebellion. I longed to see it all put right. I wanted to show them. Show them that I was just as worthy. But I could only do that in their world.

Chapter Thirteen

Land of Six Races

It was plain to see, even for a child of four: people were of all different colours. Outside on the streets and in the markets and in the shops, almost everyone was black or brown, all shades between the light brown of milky tea and deep black. Even a child of four could differentiate between Indians and Africans according to their hair: both black, but either silky or crinkly. And there were those in between, like Daddy and me who were dark, while some were fair, like Mummy, Granny Mirri, Aunt Leila, Aunt Elma, Granny Winnie, some of the uncles, and Mrs Hunter. Most of Aunt Leila's friends who came to chat in the evenings were dark-skinned, and so were most of the children I played with, the children of Aunt Leila's friends.

Race was the oversized elephant in the room in 50s BG, taking up far more space than was its due. It was a not-so-invisible spectre that invaded every interaction, that seeped into minds and twisted them a certain way, moulded them, owned them. Not many people spoke of this elephant out loud: we knew it was there, we saw it clearly, but we couldn't dispute it, couldn't banish it. It was a fact of life. The main marker of an individual's place in society.

There were other markers, too. You were slotted into your place in society not only according to the colour of your skin, but also your background, your education, your profession, your wealth, your family. But it was the colour of your skin, your race, that trumped all these in determining your value.

It was hidden in plain sight, hardly ever spoken out loud, because it was plain to see, and everyone knew it: the best thing was to be born white. It placed you at the top of the pyramid of colours and races. *Proper* white, because even those fortunate enough to be born that magical colour were divided. They weren't *proper* white if they had even a touch of another race in their ancestry – as both my grannies did – and they weren't *proper* white if they were Portuguese, because the Portuguese of BG had been brought to the colony as labourers on the sugar plantation, to replace the now emancipated Africans. So, even though the Portuguese had fair skin and soft hair, they did not count as white: they were in their own category in this land of six races.

I might only have been a small child, but I understood this clearly. These distinctions were everywhere, openly. People talked frankly about each other's skin colour and nose shape and hair quality. They described each other candidly, without malice or condescension or hatred: *'Elsie married a Black man from the East Coast. Frank's mother was an Indian, that's why he nose so straight. Patsy's children, all of them got a different colour!'*

When I was a very young child, everyday life in BG precluded meeting that exalted subset, white people. They simply did not move in our circles. I did not know anyone of that illustrious race. They were a *they*, an other, whom I encountered only in storybooks and in films, at a distance. They were a different species. What were *they* like, in real life? Were they really superior beings, different from me not only in looks, but in their entire being? If so, how come I understood the children in my books so well, could feel I was one of them? Was the difference, perhaps, only skin deep?

Even my beloved Granny Mirri acknowledged the philosophy of a racial hierarchy. As I cuddled up against her soft bosom, she'd stroke my hair and tell me I was lucky that it was soft, that my nose was straight, my lips not *too* thick and the sapodilla-brown of my skin not *too* dark.

At the same time, both Mummy and Daddy drummed it into me that everyone was of equal value, regardless of their position, status, wealth, sex, race and skin colour. That no one was better than the next person due to any of those characteristics and that it's character that counts: that what matters is who we are inside. In this and in many other areas of life, such as religion, they were already teaching me not to accept the views of the crowd. It was fine to think differently, to go against the grain, swim against the current, make up my own mind and form my own opinions.

There's no better way to do that than direct experience. And so they threw me into the fray: they thrust me into a school where 99 per cent of the other pupils were white. Only three of us at St Margaret's were dark-skinned: me, Keith and Indira, both of whom were Indian. All of a sudden I was deep in the midst of it all, a brown speck in a sea of white: learning with them, singing with them, playing with them.

St Margaret's School: Me, far left, Sheila Armstrong far right, tall Margaret (Maggie) Foreman just visible in the back row. The school building is on the right, Maggie's home behind us

It was a situation that had exactly the effect that Mummy and Daddy had hoped for. I was forced to think for myself, evaluate for myself, find out for myself. I had to ask questions, and come to my own conclusions. What makes people different? What makes them the same? What gives them value? Is it just their skin? And the more I thrived at St Margaret's, the more I saw first-hand that white children were, in reality, no different from me. They were neither better behaved nor naughtier, not more clever or more stupid, not treated differently; they didn't behave differently, think differently, speak differently. I instinctively knew that the racial hierarchy that slotted us into different levels of importance was all wrong. And I knew I could hold my own in a world of whiteness, and the colour of my skin and the texture of my hair were not things to be ashamed of. Mummy and Daddy were right: we were all of equal value.

Chapter Fourteen

Family Trees

The one-drop rule, the social and legal principle of racial classification that said that even a single 'drop' of blood from a non-white race tainted your family and lowered your social status, was very much alive in colonial BG. It meant that if you were of mixed race, you could be proud of all your Scottish, English, Dutch, German and Irish ancestors, trace them back on your family tree and learn their names. But you'd never know the names of your ancestors who were of Indian, African or Amerindian blood, and would never bother to find out those names. You didn't care about them; they were too insignificant to even be given a name, to be given a branch on the family tree. To be remembered.

I recently learned that I have Scottish ancestors: a Scottish great-great-grandfather and a Scottish great-grandfather, all on Mum's side of the family. Daddy's side is Dutch-Jewish, with a touch of Irish. But on both sides, there is also African ancestry. It is dominant. It shows. It shows in the colour of our skin and the texture of our hair and the thickness of our lips.

I know the Scottish, Dutch and Irish names: McConnell and Wight, Allicock and Hamilton, Stanton and Westmaas. I don't know a single name of a single African ancestor. These were people kidnapped from their homes and brought to the colony. They were enslaved, and forced into hard labour. They survived a horrendous journey in slave galleys, did back-breaking work on the sugar plantations from dawn to dusk. They were bought and sold as chattel, stripped of all human rights. Whipped and raped and treated as possessions, their children sold to the highest bidder. They were given English and Scottish names after the names of their white masters, and their own African names dissolved into dust, evaporated into nothing. Wiped out. Their histories erased. I have no idea who they were or where they came from, and how they made their way to British Guiana and into my family tree. I have no idea what, exactly, they suffered. I do know that they suffered. I do know that most certainly, some of them came chained down in the holds of big ships and survived the Atlantic crossing, a journey so barbarous most of their fellow captives died on the way. In their namelessness, invisible, apart from the indelible and very visible physical traces they left in our bloodline.

These ancestors exist in the shadows of the Irish, Scottish, Dutch and English who appear in the Westmaas family tree. Every now and again it mentions a 'woman of mixed blood'. But who were these women? What were their names? Where did they come from? What were their hopes and dreams? How did their blood become mixed?

As a Guianese child of mixed blood you learned, almost before you could talk, that your ancestry was split in two, down the middle. One side was good, designed to make you proud, and the other side was bad, shameful. You had to cover up the bad with the good, pretend it just wasn't there.

But your skin, your hair, your lips told a different story. Your entire body told a different story. You couldn't hide it and you certainly couldn't change it. But if you *could*; if you could only take a pill to change it, you most certainly would. You lived in the shadow of whiteness. You stayed in that shadow, knowing that white skin was the special thing, the thing that gave you worth. You saw that *they*, those superior beings with white skin, walked in the light, and you walked in their shade.

And yet, deep inside, an urgent voice cried out. Though silent, it drowned those other voices that spoke of slavery and shame: *I am! I am whole and I am good and I am right, just the way I am, no better and no worse than the exalted beings that walk in the light.* And that voice called you to come out of the shadows and just *be*, just the way you were. The way you are, here and now. If you could find it, if you could listen to it and take heart, it lifted you up and out of the shadows. That was the voice I began to hear at St Margaret's.

It wasn't a secret or an insult in BG to discuss someone's racial background or race-identifying looks. People spoke casually of hard hair, straight noses, thick lips and dark skin in critical yet non-malicious terms. They were factual but clear disadvantages you had to live with and, if possible, amend. Some women and girls – myself included, when I became more body-conscious in my teens – tried to mitigate these disadvantages with harsh chemicals on their hair, and hot-irons and even wigs. They wanted whiteness. The lighter the skin, the straighter the hair, the better you were was the conventional wisdom of the day.

It wasn't hard, even for a child, to understand that these were things that, for society, *mattered*. These were the details that secured your place in the rigid hierarchy of colonial society. You couldn't help your skin colour or nose-shape, but they placed you firmly into position, and you knew. And you had to accept that place, humbly and gracefully, never showing resentment, never complaining. But you felt it. You felt the wrongness, and it didn't only hurt. It provoked. It made some of us rebellious, determined to find another narrative. A different self-awareness.

The white bloodlines are easily traced on both sides of my family, because they are named. On the maternal side, Granny Mirri's late husband was a man of mixed blood named Walter Cox. Walter had much more than a single drop of 'tainted' blood. He had a very visible *touch of the tarbrush*, as was derogatorily said in those days, which he passed on to his four children, Mum and her two sisters, and my Uncle Percy.

And there it was in plain sight: the three firstborn girls were all fair of skin, but they had 'bad' hair, that dreaded, black and crinkly, hard-to-handle hair. Mum always wore her hair in a tidy bun on the nape of her neck, and always plaited it into two pigtails at night. It was the only way to keep it manageable. All three of Granny's daughters had this 'hard-*ish*' hair, even if their skin was fair. Uncle Percy, who lived in Trinidad, on the other hand, was dark. Dark*ish*. Not *too* dark though. Even as a young child I understood: in life, to win at the game you *had* to be white. White people were the ones of value. Superior.

Walter Cox, my grandfather, died before I was born, and his was the 'shameful' Black blood passed on to his and Granny Mirri's children. I've never seen even a photograph of him, but it must have been so. Their looks, the quality and colour of their hair, of their skin, revealed all. But, and this was the important message, he was a good man. This is all I know of him, and that's enough. Mum once said to me: 'I grew up seeing my father helping people, and I've always known that was what I wanted to do, help people.' And perhaps that is the only trait of my grandfather that I need to know: he was a good man who helped people. It is enough for me. It's a trait he passed to Mum, and the only trait that matters.

Granny Mirri herself would have been of pure English blood but for one little detail in her ancestry: her great-grandmother, an Amerindian, was adopted as a very young child by a wealthy English family named Stafford. Her name was Mary. When Mary grew up, she married a Scottish man named McConnell, who was probably related to the McConnell from Booker Brothers McConnell and Company Ltd. Mary's daughter, also called Mary, married another Scotsman named Wight. Mary Wight had several children, including my grandmother, Ruth Miriam. That little Amerindian girl, Mary Stafford, was the reason Granny Mirri could not call herself pure white. She was of mixed blood, according to the one-drop rule, even though that one drop was several generations back.

Granny Winnie, too, had married a man darker than herself and was only *almost* white, her own ancestry marred by the one-drop rule. She was descended from Robert Frederick Allicock, a Scotsman who, according to Uncle Denis's family tree, 'had thirty-two slaves and ten cows', and owned land at a place called Noitgedacht in the McKenzie area up the Demerara River. Robert married a 'woman of mixed blood' and the brown 'stain' entered the bloodline, tainting it according to the mores of the day. A few generations later, an Allicock woman married a Jewish man named James Richardson, and my grandmother, Winifred Alberta Richardson, was born. Winnie might not have been pure white, but she was certainly white enough to 'pass'.

Winnie fell in love with dark-skinned George Westmaas. The name Westmaas means 'West of the River Maas' in the Netherlands, where supposedly the name originates. My great-great-grandfather, Johannes Isaac Westmaas, was Jewish and in his early twenties he came to British Guiana, in the mid-nineteenth century, from the colony now known as Suriname. He left behind his Dutch family, who, three decades earlier, had fled the Netherlands due to the persecution of Jews. Johannes Isaac was hired, sight unseen, as the manager of Sparta Plantation in the western county of Essequibo bordering Venezuela, and stayed there throughout his life.

A few generations later, a certain George Westmaas Senior married a woman named Alicia Stenson from Kildare, Ireland. Their son George was to become my grandfather, whom we all called Pa. Alicia Stenson was therefore my great-grandmother; being Irish, she was white. Her husband George Senior, of mixed blood, was most likely dark.

George Junior, my grandfather, was also dark. He and Winnie Richardson fell in love. Winnie was a white, or white-*ish*, woman. It caused quite a ruckus in her family, for Winnie's parents disapproved entirely of such an alliance, and packed her off to Barbados to separate the two of them. But Winnie was determined; she returned to British Guiana, and sooner rather than later learned Morse code and got a job as a cable operator. And then she married her George in 1911.

Traditionally, it had always been the other way around: white men taking what they wanted from the local African or Indian woman, producing 'bastards' of mixed blood. Not in my family. On both sides, the mixed blood came through marriage, making it honourable instead. We belonged to that respectable stratum of society called the 'coloured middle class', deemed respectable because the 'tainted' blood was mixed with 'proper white' through intermarriage with the British colonisers, an uplifting, redeeming process. Colonial society was so very nuanced.

Alicia Stenson and Winnie Richardson, as well as my maternal grandmother and Mum herself, were all fair-skinned women who married dark-skinned men, women who went against the racist grain that predominated in colonial times. Women were expected and encouraged to marry 'up' the racial hierarchy, so in marrying 'down', they were rebels of a sort. They passed that rebel streak down to me. I might have still been small, but I was starting to figure out this thing called Life, and how to deal with it. I knew that something was wrong. Many things were wrong. I needed to devise a way to deal with it all.

And now, here I was at St Margaret's, one of the very few brown-skinned children in a crowd of white. And even though you knew better on the inside, the fact remained: it was better to be white. And so the brown children vied with each other as to who was the least brown. We'd place our arms together and compare: *I'm lighter! No! I am!* But we were exactly the same colour, that rich deep brown known as sapodilla-brown, because it's a similar shade to the succulent brown fruit.

It's one thing to know, intellectually, that people of all colours and races are equal. It's quite another to ignore the reality that was out there in plain sight: white people were at the top of the racial pyramid, and the lighter you were, the easier it would be to rise. It would be some time before I learned that 'easier' didn't always mean 'better'; that sometimes the hard struggles, the effort made to overcome, delivered other advantages. It gave you a toughness of character and a strength of mind you simply can't cultivate when everything falls into your lap unasked.

I was to develop that toughness in spades.

Part Two

British Guiana, 1957–61

Now I Am Nine

Chapter Fifteen

Toyland

On my sixth birthday, Mummy placed a big present in my hands and watched in delight as I tore the paper away. But then I dropped the thing as if it were a loaded bomb.

It was a doll! *A life-size baby doll!*

How could she? It was so insulting! Didn't she know me at all? I would not touch the thing. She had to return it to the shop, give it to someone else or throw it away. I didn't care, as long as it was gone. And we never spoke of the incident again.

I utterly disdained dolls, just like I disdained sticky-out frocks and frilly skirts and can-can petticoats and ribbons in my hair. It was bad enough having to wear a dress for school uniform. The frothy, pretty dresses that were the order of the day for little girls were not for me! And never, ever, did a doll cross my path again. I had better things to do in my free time than play dolly-house. There were better ways to entertain myself. And entertainment did not come from a box; neither a box containing a doll, nor a box containing a story: TV.

British Guiana did not have television, and nobody missed it. You don't miss what you've never known. Not having television meant we read more, played more, explored more, listened more, thought more about life. We made up our own entertainment. We were creative. Life was a new adventure every day, a magic faraway tree that brought new journeys and new lands to explore. We invented life anew, day by day.

We loved kites, made of coloured tissue paper glued to a cross of thin wood. Add a tail of string and rags, tie it to a long spool of twine and take it to the beach on Easter Sunday, when the sky would be dotted with hundreds of other soaring kites. The beach would be filled with children and parents, running to launch their kites, laughing, competing to see who could fly the highest, a few with razor blades attached to the tail so as to cut down rival kites. And then there were the huge box-kites, the envy of everyone, but harder to make and even harder to launch.

We made other toys. A favourite was a steamroller made of an empty thread-spool with notched rims. You threaded a rubber band through the hole in the spool and attached matches to the ends of the band to hold it in place. Then you twisted one of the matches around and around, creating a tight rubber corkscrew, and when you were ready, the little vehicle hobbled along as the rubber band unwound. We made animals out of papier mâché, and stuck leaves and flowers to paper using glue made of flour and water. We were inventive, creative, innovative, never bored for a minute.

I had a few shop-bought toys. One, when I was about three, was a red pedal motorcar, which I loved to drive around the yard. Another one, when I was older, was a wretched marionette-monkey I played with till it fell apart, inventing stimulating situations and dialogue for it. I also had a hula-hoop, and roller skates, and a scooter. I played jacks and cat's cradle and hopscotch with other children: all the traditional English games well-known all over the Empire at the time.

Then there were also those Meccano sets my cousins Ron, Wayne and Andrew played with at Granny Winnie's house. You could actually make things with them, using green metal strips, plates, wheels, axles; the nuts and bolts that connected everything, the spanners and screwdrivers to connect them all. You could make complicated buildings and vehicles that really moved, wheels that really turned, diggers that really dug. But I was much younger than my cousins, and I was a girl. They were protective of their Meccano sets and I never got to play with them on my own. At best I got to observe, and fiddle around with left-over pieces. I never thought to ask for my own set for birthday or Christmas – Meccano was clearly for boys.

But this didn't matter. I preferred insects and animals anyway, and dreaming and playing make-believe with friends, and climbing the low-hanging branches of the mango tree in the back garden, where I could sit with a book and go off into wonderful worlds of make-believe. My best friends of all were books. Stories.

I was, mostly, a solitary child. I knew how to occupy myself, and boredom or loneliness never had a chance. Nature provided umpteen miracles in the huge backyard, and books provided adventures galore.

It all began with bedtime, that special time for Mum and me. Cuddled in the big bed we shared, enclosed in the white mosquito net tucked all around the mattress, she'd tell me stories made up on the spot, stories about talking mice and runaway children on British Guiana's back-dam or shorefront. And therein, perhaps, lay my future. Stories came alive in my mind, drew me into new worlds, worlds without boundaries where whatever I wanted could happen.

Once I learned to write myself, I'd sit at my little desk in my upstairs room and fill one exercise book after another with stories. I wrote stories of children going off on fabulous adventures, children with horses and dogs. My imagined children found buried treasure and brought thieves and evil kidnappers to justice. They always lived in England à la Famous Five, because that's where all the best adventures happened, the adventures I wanted to have. And their skin was always white, like all the children in all the books I read.

The characters I made up were my friends; I gave them names, gave them pets and ponies and adventures I could not have myself. I thought of them as real, alive; children who had wonderful adventures in faraway places. How I envied those fortunate children!

How I longed to be like them, to play with them, to join them on their adventures! But I could only do so in imagination. And imagination ran away with me.

I learned to create my own worlds and my own fictional friends, and that's what made life in a house full of adults quite tolerable, and a life in Lamaha Street very close to paradise.

We humans have a built-in affinity for storytelling. It is through storytelling that we best learn the important lessons that life has to teach us. It is through stories, rather than lectures, that we learn morality and ethics. While films and television can provide the pictures that accompany those stories, make them come to life for us, they are really a shortcut; they eliminate that vital process by which we create those stories in our own minds. Without a screen we have to create those pictures ourselves, 'see' them internally. We make up the mental images to go along with the stories, rather than have them delivered, ready-made, into our minds.

People these days speak of the 1950s in denigrating terms. But to me, they were heaven on earth. Never was a time so free, so liberating. Never was a place so all-embracing, so *motherly*, for a child as 50s British Guiana. It folded itself around you and filled you with a sense of deep comfort, a sense of well-being that held you safe, replete with a quiet happiness that depended on nothing more than simply being alive.

Chapter Sixteen

How Much Is That Doggie in the Window?

In a corner of the drawing room at Lamaha Street there was a polished wood cabinet on which stood the oversized radio, a big beast of a thing. You could twiddle its knobs and watch the line marching across a screen, across the world even, picking up voices in strange languages from far-off countries. Truly, the world was at my feet with that radio.

Next to the radio sat the record player, and below that on a built-in shelf, the pile of records, 45s and 33-and-a-thirds. 'Handle them with care!' Aunt Leila would warn, and I did. That meant only ever to hold the records secured between the palms of my hands; never to touch their delicate surfaces, because, once scratched, they were ruined forever; to carefully place the needle on the spinning rim, and never, ever to touch its tip, because I might not only injure myself, but injure *it* as well.

I learned to carefully replace the needle if it grew wobbly or dull, and to manage that pile of records, because nobody else in the house was interested.

I played those records until I knew the songs off by heart: 'Three Coins In The Fountain', 'How Much Is That Doggie In The Window?', 'Tulips From Amsterdam'... A great favourite was Elvis Presley's 'Wooden Heart'. I was fascinated by the German words at the end of it. I'd sing, loud and clear: *woosie denn, woosie den, owsden shtate-elly-hinaws, shtate-elly-hinaws, undo mine shats blys here*, and with that, I convinced myself I knew a bit of German.

*

I was eager to learn French, and Mum immediately proceeded to teach me. She bought me a book called *French Without Tears*, and I learned the first lesson by heart. It was a text about a boy called Robert and another boy called Charles. Robert was big and Charles was small, and Robert had Charles's penknife. *Où est le canif de Charles?* were among my first French words, never to be forgotten, along with the *je t'aime beaucoup* Dad had taught me in London.

Thanks to me, the gramophone or the radio blared all day when I was in the house, filling it with the Pat Boone and Elvis Presley hits of the day. But if I fiddled enough with the dials on the radio I'd find various American children's programmes. My favourite was Art Linkletter's 'Kids Say the Darndest Things', a segment from his popular show *House Party*. Linkletter interviewed thousands of children between the ages of five and ten, and I found it hilarious.

What would you like to be?

A stewardess.

What if a plane was in danger over the Rocky Mountains?

I'd put parachutes on everybody and if there wasn't any parachutes I'd sew up sheets into parachutes real fast and put in extra pillows so if the sheets ripped on the way down, they could always land on the pillows.

Yes! That's exactly what I'd do too. I used to eye the wardrobe in my bedroom and try to figure out ways to climb up there so I could jump down, using an umbrella as a parachute. I tried pushing a chair close to the wardrobe but it was no good; I was still too far from the top. The Lamaha Street house had no ceiling, so there was lots of space over our heads to practise jumping down, not only from the tops of wardrobes but from the rafters in the open roof and the tops of walls as well. I was sure it would work. After all, my intrepid older cousin Wayne had also tried jumping, from increasing heights, with a bedsheet as a parachute. I'd watched him closely and knew it was possible.

Later, when we stayed with Uncle Percy in Port-of-Spain, I'd peer down from my window on the first floor and try to convince my mother to let me jump to the ground. *It's not really high, Mummy! I'm sure I can do it!* But she never let me. Mum did not have many rules, and seldom laid down the law. But jumping out of the first-floor window was one freedom I was not allowed. I discovered the library instead. I'd go there and return with piles of Enid Blyton novels.

If I was lucky, Mummy or Daddy would actually buy me a new book. There was only one bookshop, in Bookers Universal Store, right next to the snack bar. Whenever Aunt Leila took me shopping, that's where she would park me, and that's where I'd wait for her, browsing, checking out the newest arrivals, making a list in my head for what I could request next at the library. It was books, books, books. Magic could be found in a book, and new worlds, and new existences. As long as I had a book, I was happy. A good book was even more important than ants and tadpoles. Lost in books, that was my world from as soon as I could read.

But I also loved comics, starting with the comic strips in all the newspapers. Some of the papers would have a whole page of a supplement dedicated to comic strips. I read them all: Mutt and Jeff, Archie, Dennis the Menace, Blondie and Dagwood, Peanuts, Mickey Mouse, Donald Duck and the entire Disney family. I'd be the first to grab the papers and extract the comics page.

But best of all were the comic *books* you could buy at any of the shops. Whole stories, told in pictures! My favourites included Little Lulu, Casper the Friendly Ghost with his nemesis Spooky, Archie,

Betty and Veronica, Superman, Supergirl, Batman and Spider-Man. Later on, as my taste in comics grew more sophisticated, there was Schoolgirls' Picture Library, Cowboy Picture Library, and later yet, Romance Picture Library. These were smaller comic books, smaller even than real books, and you could subscribe to them and they'd be sent to you. I devoured them.

But of course, a comic book could hardly compare to an animated cartoon on a cinema screen. My first memory of a cartoon was, once again, in London, with Tweety Bird indelibly merged in my mind.

Mum never read novels or went to the cinema; she was pragmatic in temperament, and beyond making up little bedtime stories for a sleepy daughter, she didn't waste her time with such frivolities. She left the cinema-going bit to Dad, and it was he who took me to see films most weekends, in one of our several cinemas: the Plaza, the Metropole, the Globe or the Empire. They showed all the Disney films of the era, as well as the comedies we loved: Laurel and Hardy, the Marx Brothers and Jerry Lewis. Dad and I would laugh our heads off in the darkness of the cinema.

And then there were action films: cowboy shows such as Roy Rogers and his faithful horse Trigger, and, of course, his sidekick Tonto, all of whom only helped to embed the love of horses in my little mind. Other favourites were Lassie, and Tarzan. We went to see *Old Yeller*, about the dog who caught rabies and had to be put down, which broke my heart. I cried for days.

We went to the cinema frequently, but it was always a great occasion for which you dressed up smartly. There were always two films at every showing, and invariably there'd be the pre-show features. First came 'God Save the Queen'. The Queen would ride majestically onto the big screen on her beautiful shiny steed, and the entire audience would rise to its feet. Yes, even my radically anti-imperialist, pro-Marxist father.

After the Queen had saluted the flag, having done our civic duty we'd all settle back into our seats for the Pathé News, which showed us what was going on all over the British Empire. Then came the cartoons: usually Mickey Mouse or Donald Duck. And then, at last, the first feature. In the pause between the two features we could get up and stretch our legs, and buy snacks and soft drinks and discuss what we'd seen. All in all, going to the cinema would be a special treat lasting many delicious hours. And for Dad and me, it was an outing that cemented our relationship.

Dad had some favourite adult films of his own, but he shared them with me through their music, and I knew them through their signature songs. I may even have watched them with him. *Oklahoma!* was one, with 'Oh, What a Beautiful Mornin', and 'Thank Heaven for Little Girls' from *Gigi*. I have a distinct memory of Maurice Chevalier singing that to a little girl on the big screen, and I remember that top hat. How Dad loved singing those songs to me. They reflected, to my mind, the sentimental side of my dad. The warm and loving side, which to my childlike mind, seemed so in contrast to the other dad. The militant revolutionary dad, the dad who used big words I couldn't understand, and who tried to teach me about grown-up matters I was still too small to comprehend. Dad had a strong didactic vein to his personality. Raising a child, to him, was a matter of guiding it along the right path, teaching it the right way to think, move, and have its being.

Mum was the opposite. She didn't regard it as her role to tell me what to do or how to think. She wanted freedom for me. Hers was the quintessential laissez-faire method of raising a child, and she allowed me to figure it all out by myself. She reckoned, I believe, that I would take her as a model for right living. That I would see and learn, and find my way. She would *show* me how to live rather than *tell* me. The way she did this was to let me go on a loose rein, trusting that I would find my way in the end.

From the youngest age, I knew Mum as the role model in whose steps I should follow, and I couldn't have had a better one. Some people might call her ascetic, but that's what I liked most about her, the example I most wanted to live up to, but never could. Perhaps her example was too high for me to reach. Perhaps being raised on too loose a leash made me sloppy and intemperate.

Whatever it was, to me she was perfect. Modest and unpretentious to a fault, integrity and maturity ran through her veins. She was pretty but lacked even a sliver of vanity. She never cared about fashion, or primping herself. Her dress style was simple and functional; her outward appearance was clean, tidy and practical rather than attractive. She wore flat shoes and no make-up, always smart and trim. On her dressing table stood, throughout the years, a hairbrush and comb, a photo of me aged three, and a bottle of Oil of Olay, the only skincare product she ever used. To complete her well-groomed look, a box of face powder and a powder puff. That was all.

After her divorce she was not interested in finding a new mate, and made no effort to be appealing to men. Genuinely content as a single working mother, she took back her maiden name and the title Miss. She did not flirt, nor play mating games. She held no secret hankering for a new husband. This self-sufficiency revealed itself in every aspect of her private life, and echoed into external details. Her handwriting was small and rounded, precise and easily legible, as was her signature, always in full: Eileen R. Cox. No scribbles or scrawls for her. She kept her correspondence well ordered, in files. She typed almost all of her letters, never making a mistake, and made duplicates even of personal letters, keeping those duplicates in a separate file. Carbon paper was her best friend.

Financially, too, she was organised. She abhorred debt, and was well aware of the power of banks to exploit their customers. *Join the credit union!* was the financial advice she gave me from a young age. *Save as much as you can! Don't waste your money!* It was sound advice that, throughout my younger days, went in my left ear and out the right. I only learned to appreciate her advice as a mature adult; too late, some would say. As a result, *you think money grows on trees!* became another frustrated cry of hers in my later years.

Towards men she remained friendly but distant, always self-assured and never compliant, highly critical yet disarming. They seemed in awe of her. I know of more than one man who was secretly in love with her, more than one who'd say 'how high?' when she said 'jump'. But Mum remained serenely single. She never had a boyfriend after her divorce, never dated, never showed any interest in a second marriage or even a romantic fling. She was good enough for herself: self-contained, moral and just, yet never judgemental or prissy, never boring or bored. She was everything I wanted to be, but couldn't.

I had two excellent parents, and I was a dry sponge placed in their hands. I watched and listened and tried to figure it all out, navigate between Dad's maxims and formulas for a life of integrity, and Mum's freedoms and her living example of what was a good, honourable human being. I had to find a middle way, pick and choose the right path for me. I fumbled my way through, fell often, picked myself up again and again. Life, I eventually concluded, was not about seeking pleasures but about learning to live, to love, and to grow along the way. That's the way to a truly happy life. Most importantly, I learned – eventually – not to follow and accept blindly what others do and think, but to decide my own actions for myself, in keeping with my conscience.

Chapter Seventeen

Celebrations

The following Christmas, Mum made up for the dolly debacle with the best present ever. I must have been seven. Even now, I remember coming down the stairs and seeing it there, propped up on its stand next to the gaily decorated Christmas tree, not even wrapped up because it was too big. A bicycle! A real red bicycle, a Hercules! I flung my arms around her in gratitude, and rushed to start riding it around the room; I had already learned to ride at Crown Street. Daddy had taught me, on one of the many children's bikes there. And now I had one of my own.

It was Christmas, a BG Christmas, the most glorious of seasons. We put up Christmas trees each year, as everyone did. There they stood, all lit up in the windows of every home, and we'd drive around town just to count them and admire the lights strung up in all the houses. The trees, of course, were all artificial. Firs and pines don't grow in Guyana. After the Christmas season, the trees and lights would be folded up and packed away for the next year.

In the run-up to Christmas Aunt Leila would take me window-shopping. The two main stores, Bookers and Fogarty's, all had magnificent displays in their windows, and I loved nothing better than to walk along the pavements, hand in hand with Aunty, or hooked into her elbow, and peer into them: it all seemed so magical!

Both stores had their own Santa Claus, who would sit on a throne in the midst of a landscape of billowing white cotton wool. A man with a brown face in a red suit that must have had him sweating rivers. We children lined up to get to sit on his lap and he'd give us a present (prepaid by our adults) and say 'Ho! Ho! Ho!' before the next child was summoned. The presents were mostly useless. I always got a dolly, which I'd never touch. Presumably Aunt Leila passed them on to some other little girl who knew how to be thankful.

Our two radio stations, Radio Demerara and British Guiana Broadcasting Service (BGBS), blared out Christmas songs, day and night, and nobody cared that they were highly inappropriate for the equatorial climate: 'Frosty the Snowman', 'Rudolph, The Red-Nosed Reindeer', 'White Christmas', and, the mother of them all, 'Jingle Bells'. Who cared that no Guyanese child would ever go dashing through the snow in a one-horse open sleigh? That we didn't ever dream of a white Christmas, or build a snowman? The music brought with it feelings. Good feelings.

Those light-hearted songs held great magic for us all, but the carols even more so. We'd have carol singers, groups of people, mostly women and girls, who walked the streets for an evening singing all the familiar carols: 'O Come, All Ye Faithful'; 'Deck The Halls'; 'Hark! The Herald Angels Sing'; 'Away In A Manger'; 'God Rest Ye Merry, Gentlemen'. These singers literally served up good cheer. We'd stand at the windows or on the front porch or stairs and listen, enthralled, and then somebody would go down and put something in the collection box. And there'd be that cosy, mellow, glorious Christmassy feel that comes but once a year. Even I, a child raised atheist, adored it; there was something sweet and indescribable about it, a warmth that spread through your very being, body and soul, and we all basked in it, Christian or not. Even Hindus and Muslims took part in the festivities: Christmas cheer and goodwill was for everyone. It was the best feeling of all. Even Daddy did not dare to ban Christmas, and against his most adamant will for me not to be indoctrinated, I learned the

Christmas story about the birth of Jesus. And, against his expressed demand for me to reject it all, I loved it. It was the best story of all.

The total immersion in Christmas music formed the very essence of that precious Christmas feeling. Absorbed into young, impressionable minds in childhood, it coalesces into a lifelong nostalgia, a sentimentality that is not at all tacky, but precious, healing. A yearning for a wholesome world, a wholesome life, a wholesome me. I had it in spades, and still do; a sense of an unbelievable, miraculous goodness, which practically rushed in to fill all the vacuums in my being. I challenge anyone who knew that feeling as a child to deny its power. Dad was fighting a losing battle. Not even he, with his atheism and scepticism, could destroy that most glorious of seasons.

But there are certain Guyanese people, older people in the diaspora especially, who'll claim it's not the music that brings on that sweet nostalgia, but the food. In the months, weeks and days before Christmas, housewives would be falling over themselves in their kitchens to prepare their feasts, soaking fruit in rum months ahead to make the magnificent black cake, based, I suspect, on English Christmas pudding. And on Christmas Day itself there'd be pepper-pot, which consisted of beef and pork, black with the indigenous Amerindian seasoning cassareep; or garlic pork. I'm told that these two dishes are absolute heaven on earth, but I wouldn't know, as I never tried them. I am a picky eater, remember? But I loved fruit of course! At Christmas it was apples and pears, specialities imported from England only at this time of year. And cheese, great balls of Edam enclosed in red wax, which we called Dutchman's Head. Apples, pears, and Edam: those were my Christmas delicacies.

To drink, we had the tree-bark-based beverage mauby, fresh juices and, for the adults, rum in everything. A day for families to gather, for men to get drunk and mothers to run in circles herding children and feeding everyone.

Presents were never the main attraction at Christmas. I only wanted books, but had to tolerate, with polite thanks, a few packets of new knickers from various aunties. Knickers, known as panties, were a staple present for girls on birthdays or at Christmas. Granny Winnie gave me a tin of Cadbury's chocolates every year – and I suspect she gave the same to all her grandchildren. It was a cream-coloured, tall oval tin, and the first thing I'd do was pick out my favourites, the walnut swirls, and gobble them up. Yes, I was a picky eater, but I still had my sweet tooth, and you could always win me over with chocolate. Sometimes there were bigger presents. I must have been four when I got my little red pedal car, which I adored. And then, wonder of wonders: that beautiful new Hercules bike.

After I got my bike, Georgetown was my oyster. I rode it everywhere: to school around the corner in Camp Street, to visit friends, and even across town to my other granny's house in Crown Street, Queenstown.

Then there was Easter, and Good Friday, when the entire country fell into a reverent silence. A kind of holy trance, in which you had to watch your language, your behaviour and your moods, and align them with the gravity of the day. Even non-Christians respected the sanctity of Good Friday. We non-aligned citizens, big and small, felt it in our bones and our blood. Today was the day Christ was crucified. That needed to be honoured with every breath we took, whether we called ourselves Christian or not.

And then came Easter Sunday! Jubilation! Church bells ringing out: *He is Risen!* Joy and Celebration! Bring out your kites, children, and let's all go down to the beach and raise them up. Let the sky be filled with brilliantly coloured symbols of freedom, of resurrection, of renewal. Raise your kite to the sky, and rejoice, for *He is Risen!* The crowded beach, the crowded sky, hot cross buns and an Easter feast, and all things good. Christmas and Easter, the two great celebrations of the year. Both my parents were helpless against the force of those seasons, unable to pour the cold water of rationality over the symbolism. Dad even made Easter kites for me. Kites were, after all, secular things.

Chapter Eighteen

The Grim Reaper

Granny Winnie's face in my memory is always a face distorted by grief. When I was just seven, tragedy struck our family. My cousin Wayne – one of the half-orphans Granny was raising – loved experimenting with chemicals in the downstairs room. One day I returned from the playground to see him running around the corner of the house, clutching his chest, blood spurting through his fingers and running down his shirt. He collapsed in the front yard.

After that everything happened in a chaotic whirr. Screams and shouts and people panicking. Wayne's father, Uncle Rupert, bundling him into Dad's Ford Prefect, Dad leaping into the driver's seat. Dad racing off, Uncle Rupert in the back, cradling Wayne in his arms. Off they sped towards the hospital.

But Wayne was dead on arrival. Back at home, we all waited for news, stunned and shocked. People from the neighbourhood heard what had happened and came rushing up. Adults, mostly women, standing around, weeping, wailing, hugging. Wide-eyed children, lost for words, struck dumb by the atmosphere of adult shock and cold sheer dread. At last, the car returned. Dad got out and rushed into the bottom flat he shared with his wife Faye, weeping. I followed, a little shadow, unable to grasp the implication of what had just happened, still trying to process that image of Wayne running towards me with blood gushing from his chest.

Dad flung himself on to a bed, heaving with sobs. Me, I did not cry. I was only seven. I was more shocked at Dad crying than at Wayne's death.

Later, we learned what had happened to Wayne: a pipe-bomb, held the wrong way round, had exploded into his heart. Later still, my cousin Ron, Wayne's big brother, explained the details to me. At the time, there was a craze among kids for making small 'bombs' with home-made gunpowder made from simple chemicals bought at the local chemists. They would pack this in small tins, light the fuse and run. Once before, when Wayne had been making up this explosive, a small quantity had ignited and singed his hair. Apparently, he said, 'The experiment must go on.' Typically, Wayne then took things further and attempted to make a small cannon, a pipe-bomb. He held it the wrong way around and it went off into his heart.

Wayne was one of those Westmaases with a reputation for being, to put it politely, *unconventional*. He had a lively imagination and would get up to all sorts of mischief. Once, when Uncle Rory was politically active, the Crown Street house was surrounded and being searched for 'subversive literature' by the police as well as by heavily armed Argyll and Sutherland Highlanders. Uncle Rupert, Wayne's father, caught Wayne creeping down the back stairs with his toy bow and arrow, intent on shooting a soldier. Terrified, Rupert grabbed Wayne and dragged him back into the house.

Eccentrics, non-conformists, radicals: that's what they called us, mostly fondly. The Westmaases had a tendency to swim against the flow, to not fit into the mainstream. Wayne belonged in this category but this time, he took things a little too far and paid the ultimate price.

I will never forget Granny's face the day they brought Wayne home and laid him there in the front room, cold and stiff and pale.

I will never forget the atmosphere in the house of cold, blank grief. The house, the whole neighbourhood, fell into a state of deep shock.

Dad, a confirmed atheist, had always told me there was no heaven and hell, that death was the end of a natural process and nothing to be afraid of. Death was normal, and humans only turned to religion because of the fear of death. Yet here he was, sobbing like a child. Here were all the adults, paralysed by grief, everyone crying. Adults didn't cry! Dads didn't cry! But cry they all did.

Wayne's was not the first death I'd experienced first-hand. Pa, Dad's father, had died the year before, when I was six. My only memory of him is of his body lying in a coffin.

This was in 1958, when a visiting Princess Margaret passed by the Crown Street house, waving back to all the people lining the streets, cheering through a sea of Union Jacks. The excitement must have been too much for Pa, who was sitting, as usual, in his rocking chair in the gallery. He had a seizure, possibly a stroke, after she passed by and died a few days later. He'd been quite active until right before his collapse, but had been having treatment for some years for a heart condition.

I saw Pa dead. It was my first glimpse of human death, my first taste of the finality of death. There he reposed, in his coffin, lying in state throughout the wake. A sense of coldness washed through me as I regarded the corpse. The strange waxy pallor of the skin; my total awareness that this body was just an empty vessel; that its essence, the life that had filled it, was gone. Where to? How could someone just *cease to exist*, from one day, one moment, to the next? Where did the life go, the life that had once filled that body?

I asked myself these questions but had no answers, beyond what Daddy told me: *Death is the end. We have to accept it. People invent God and heaven through fear of death, instead of facing it realistically. They invent an afterlife as comfort, and build religions to contain that myth. But there is no God, no heaven. There is only this, our one life, which is finite. That's it. That's all there is.*

Dad always had a wise word, an astute aphorism, a rational explanation to hand. He always tried to help me understand the world, in language a six-year-old could understand. I had not yet learned to doubt him. Pa was dead, and there he lay, pale and cold.

And now, Wayne. Yes, I'd seen Pa's body, but I'd been too young to grasp what had happened, and anyway, Pa had been *old*. Old people die, even I knew that. Wayne was young. Much too young to be ripped away from us. Not a distant grandfather I could hardly remember, but my cousin, a friend, someone I knew. A boy who only a few days before had been a rascally, boisterous barrel of fun, always up to some mischief or the other. How could he lie there, still and cold, dead?

What is death? Where do we go? I understood we all have to die, but how was it possible to simply *stop*, just like that? How could thoughts, feelings, a personality, a whole life lived, simply come to an end? There had to be more, I thought. We couldn't just *stop*, full stop. Life was life, and even Daddy, big strong Daddy, who had an answer to everything and scoffed at death and said it was nothing, was there blubbering like a child.

Wayne was fourteen when he died, and I was seven. Too young to understand the enigma of death, but old enough to comprehend the hole left in a family when the Grim Reaper attacks. I felt the cold fingers of dread as my own heart felt the loss.

They brought Wayne's body home and laid it in the gallery. It was not Wayne. It was just a white cold body, empty of life. I stared at it, filled with a macabre fascination. Granny sat beside the body in her rocking chair. Rocking back and forth, silent. Her face was unrecognisable, carved with a grief unfathomable for a child of seven. Granny had been Wayne's mother figure for most of his life. I had questions, but the Westmaas adults, even Uncle Denis, were too consumed by grief to pay me or my questions any attention. As for Mum, she simply never spoke of such matters, not even when Wayne died. I was left on my own, to figure it all out myself, when confronted with life's greatest mystery.

Later, Granny Winnie's memory started to fail, and so did her grasp of names. The names of all her sons would roll off her tongue as she tried to find the right one: 'Denis-David-Donald-Douglas-Rupert-Patrick-Leonard-Rory!' They all must have merged into one for her, with one common multiple name.

But one by one, she lost them. One son, Donald, married in England after the war and never returned to Guyana. With one exception – Uncle Denis – the others married and had children, and in the late 50s and the 60s the exodus began. One after the other, family by family, Granny's sons emigrated, taking their wives and children with them. Almost all flew or sailed away, seeking the greener fields of Britain, Canada and the US.

The Crown Street house gradually emptied. The only brothers who remained in those early years were Uncle Denis and Dad, though Uncle Rory did return later on. The Westmaas family, once a close-knit unit with a well-known name in Georgetown, was now scattered across three continents, and Granny a forgetful, wrinkled old woman in the Crown Street house, playing 'Danny Boy' on the violin, attended to by her one bachelor son, Denis.

But Granny had once been a young woman with dreams and aspirations of her own, a mother who had raised eight healthy sons and five healthy grandchildren. And Wayne's death was not the first shattering loss in her life. In 1939 war broke out in Europe. While young men back in the United Kingdom were being drafted into military service, no such obligation existed in British Guiana. Yet four of Granny's sons volunteered, and off they went: David, Denis, Rory and Douglas. Donald served in the Home Guard. Dad was in the RAF.

The Westmaas soldiers, left to right David (Daddy), Douglas, Denis, Rory

What must it be like for a mother to send half her sons off to fight a war half a world away? It is unimaginable. Yet she must also have been proud. One of my memories of the Crown Street house is of a wall covered with framed photos of her sons in uniform. Soldier boys, all so handsome, eyes alight with eagerness to do their bit. My own dad in his RAF uniform, in my eyes the handsomest of them all. Who would not be proud?

One day later in the war, Granny, her husband George and other family members were at lunch when a crash startled them all. The photo of Uncle Douglas had fallen off the wall, crashed to the floor, its glass shattered. 'Douglas is dead!' cried Granny Winnie. And it was true. On 14 February 1942, the warship carrying Corporal Douglas Ivan Westmaas of the Royal Corps of Signals unit was torpedoed by the Japanese off the coast of Singapore. His name is engraved on the Commonwealth War Dead Memorial in Singapore.

Chapter Nineteen

Myths and White Rabbits

'There's no God!' Daddy told me, time and time again. That was the main, most important, lesson I had to learn. 'God is a figment of man's imagination. Religion was invented to enslave us. Religion is the opium of the people. Prayer is useless. There's no heaven or hell! It's all a myth!'

Dad passed his wisdom on to me from the youngest age. It was, basically, an indoctrination against indoctrination. *Don't let them brainwash you!* he would warn me, again and again.

The trouble was, I was *not* being brainwashed. Nobody was teaching me to be a good Christian, least of all Mum, who was an agnostic and simply let me be. There were no religion classes at St Margaret's – or if there were, I must have been excused from them, for I have no memory of them. An exemption from religious classes is just the kind of thing Dad – and Mummy too – would have insisted on.

I did not go to church, or Sunday School. I was not baptised. But once I took part in a school nativity play. I was an angel, with wings Aunt Leila had made for me from a can-can petticoat pinned to my back, with elastic bands attaching the skirt to my wrists so that, arms raised, my wings spread out. One cheeky little shepherd boy pointed and laughed: 'You should be wearing that under your skirt,' he said. I wanted to sink into the floor in shame. But I was a compliant child; I fluttered around as an angel, and never wore a can-can again.

The closest I came to a religious education was through Aunt Leila, but even then, only through observation. Aunt Leila was very devout. She subscribed to a small booklet called the *Daily Word*, which published Bible quotes and inspirational messages and instructions for every day, which she read religiously. She'd then sit on the side of her bed, palms open on her knees, eyes closed, and meditate.

This fascinated me. What was she doing? What was she thinking? What was going on? I knew not to interrupt her when she did this, and I never asked. But I was curious. She also went to church on Sundays, along with Aunt Edna. She never told me anything about her Christianity, never tried to win me for Christ, never tried to influence me. That may have been according to Mummy's orders. If Mummy had told her I was not to have a religious education, Aunt Leila would never have interfered.

I did however hear a rumour that she, together with Dad's brother Denis, had secretly baptised me when I was a baby. A Catholic friend told me it was probably true: she would have worried about my immortal soul, in case I died early, and wanted to protect it. Uncle Denis, a devout Christian, might very well have teamed up with her for a clandestine baptism; he and Dad were often at loggerheads on religion.

In spite, or maybe because, of Dad's insistence that there was no God, I was curious. I looked around me and wondered. Where did it all come from? Why were there people on earth? What was the reason for everything? Why were there flowers, and animals, and food to eat – fruits, so delicious your mouth watered even at the thought of them? What about the night sky filled with stars, which when you looked up at it filled you with awe? What about the sun, rising religiously and gloriously each day, giving life? What about babies, miraculously growing in their mummies' tummies until they popped out, whole and perfect? Why, why, why?

I now had a real-life baby to ponder, my little stepbrother Nigel. A baby was such a miraculous thing! How did it happen? How did it know how to grow, and so perfectly? Where did I come from? Who am I? It seemed strange that all this should just happen randomly. It seemed like a miracle.

'Everything can be explained by science,' Daddy told me, and went on to explain what science was. His explanation was not satisfactory, because the next question was who, or what, made science? Why? What was the source?

The more Dad tried to cleanse my mind of any notion of God – a notion that wasn't actually there to begin with – the more curious I became, and the more I thought about the concept, and what it meant. In arguing against the existence of God, Dad actually put the very notion of creation, and a power behind it all, into my little head. I looked around me, and pondered.

Then a strange thing happened. Whenever I thought of God, or even thought the word *God*, a wondrous sense would overcome me. A sense I had no word for, and only later could give a name to. It was a feeling of overwhelming awe, an awe so great, I'd almost shudder with raw emotion, and withdraw from the thought. It seemed to me a word so great, so overpowering, it should not even be spoken out loud, and not bandied about, and even disparaged, the way Dad did. It was too big a concept to even contemplate. So I didn't.

Mummy, on the other hand, never spoke of God, neither confirmed nor denied the existence of such a power. If put on the spot, she'd say, 'We just don't know.' But like Dad, she wanted me to be raised without religious dogma, free of the opium of the people, free from the very concept of religion.

Chapter Twenty

All the -Isms

Atheism wasn't the only -ism I had to deal with. There were many others, from both of my parents and many of the grown-ups who surrounded me. There were so many words I didn't understand. I'd listen in to adult conversations, at both grannies' houses, but I couldn't follow. So many words, so many -isms.

With Mum it was feminism, trade unionism, consumerism, agnosticism, humanism. I couldn't even pronounce the words and I had no idea what they meant, but it was clear that they were important things because she was always talking about them, with her friends, on the phone or with anyone who would listen. She was so passionate about these -isms, and sometimes tried to explain them to me, but I didn't understand at all. Did feminism mean that mothers couldn't be with their children? Is that why Aunt Leila took care of me and cooked for me? Because she wasn't a feminist? Did that make her a bad person? I just didn't get it.

It was the same with Daddy, but with other isms: Marxism, communism, socialism, colonialism, expansionism, imperialism and, of course, atheism. And let's not forget humanism, just like Mummy.

I just didn't understand big-people talk. It's politics, Daddy told me. I didn't like politics. It made grown-ups so angry. My adored, fun-loving dad became a different man when he spoke politics. Especially when he spoke politics with Uncle Rory.

Uncle Rory was the one. Whenever I meet a Guyanese person anywhere in the world and tell them my last name, that's the question they shoot back: any relation to Rory? And I can proudly say: yes. Rory was my uncle.

We were all proud of our Uncle Rory. As a child, that pride was best summed up in this announcement, told to anyone who asked: *I have an uncle who went to jail!* Uncle Rory having been in jail was a badge of honour. I had no idea, at the time, what it was all about, but I knew he was a hero, and that he did us proud. And so I too was proud. His was the kind of detainment anyone would be proud of.

The early 1950s in Guyana, then British Guiana, was a boiling hotbed of political activity, with volatile and outspoken sections of society rising up to challenge the colonial state. Uncle Rory was foremost among these dissidents, an outspoken member of a small radical group vehemently against the stranglehold of Great Britain on the colony.

At only seven, I had no idea what was going on, of course. I only knew that it had to do with those terrible things: colonialism and imperialism, words I heard on a daily basis without knowing their meanings. And I knew that Uncle Rory was a great hero for standing up for the people of our country, and that the British hated him and had thrown him into jail. Even in appearance, he was impressive; tall, lanky and good-looking, like all the Westmaas men, he sported a well-clipped beard and looked the very image of a revolutionary.

As for me, Uncle Rory is the uncle I remember best, the one I looked up to in sheer awe. But he was not just a dissident: he was also a family man, a householder, and an architect who taught at the University of Guyana for over thirty years. He was a man decades before his time. I remember once asking for his advice on renovating my mother's Subryanville house, which was barely a hundred metres from the sea. He said, 'Don't do it. The entire coastland is endangered; the sea is going to rise, and the house will be under water.' This was back in the early 2000s, long before climate change became a watchword in the West.

One of the ways in which Uncle Rory stood out for me was in the naming of his children: Storm, Blaze, Peter and Wilde, all very unconventional names for the time. 'Blaze' is actually spelled Blaise, 'Wilde' is spelled Wylde, and 'Peter', a girl, is actually spelled Peta, but I didn't know this as a child. Decades before gender-neutral and non-traditional names for offspring became a trend, we had a girl phonetically called Peter in the family. Uncle Rory was a model of living life against the grain. Like Mum, he was far ahead of his time.

Mum, meanwhile, was forging ahead with her own -isms. The party-politics of her ex-husband and his revolutionary brother Rory were not for her. Instead, Mum worked from the bottom up: with women struggling for equal rights, with trade unionists struggling for worker rights. She supported small farmers and local businesses and she detested anything that smelled of a monopoly. She disdained big business, and millionaires whose wealth had been built on the backs of the poor and at the expense of society's health. She thought the men at the top of these organisations were liars and scoundrels, not to be trusted. Attributes such as wealth and high birth did not impress her; if your wealth was earned at the expense of others, in her eyes you were toast, and she would let you know it. She fought battles for the underdog, and mostly won those battles. She was most passionate about women's rights, and fought with all her might to raise the status of women in the colony, both at work and in the home; to protect them from overbearing men who rode roughshod over them.

She didn't only fight with words and legalese. She was a hands-on activist, and any woman who needed an ear and a shoulder to cry on, legal advice, or a spokeswoman against the authorities: there she was. Many a time in my childhood, I was jealous of strangers because they seemed to occupy more of my mother's time and attention than I did. And at the same time, I was immensely proud of her, and knew she was the model I had to live up to, but never could. I later understood why she had turned down the national scholarship, the chance to rise up the ranks herself: as a government minister, her hands would have been tied. As a committed individual, working on her own initiative for the good of others, she was free from outside influence, lobbyists and other coercive powers. She fought her battles with great determination, forcefully yet politely.

And Mum was always polite. She always stated her case calmly and decisively, knowing she was simply *right*, and never feeling the need for anger or for aggression. She never swore, she never shouted. I never heard her raise her voice in anger, or use a curse word. Though often frustrated by male arrogance, she did not hate or fear men, nor cede an inch to them.

Inexplicably, men listened to her. It was as if she had a secret weapon, subtly wielded, that kept them firmly in their place. Even when up in arms she was disarming and, somehow, men respected her. In every photo I have of her from that time, all the men seem to be smiling docilely, almost deferentially, at her. There are photos of her sitting confidently and calmly in the midst of a group of men, not in the least perturbed at being the only woman. Mum rose above all the -isms with stalwart personal engagement, and over the years became a household name, known and almost revered in every section of society. She became a hero, an icon – and on her own terms. She eventually resigned from her final role as founder and president of the Guyana Consumer Association at the exalted age of ninety-three with all her marbles intact.

Chapter Twenty-One

Sproston's Dock House

I no longer walked to school with Aunt Leila, I rode my lovely new red bicycle instead. I loved school. I loved reading and art best of all, but I had a small problem that would eventually grow into a big problem. I didn't like talking. I never raised my hand in class because I didn't want to speak, because the sound of my own voice bothered me, embarrassed me. And there was a reason for that reluctance to let others, apart from close family and childhood friends, hear me talk. I was, quite literally, tongue-tied. A short, tight piece of skin attached my tongue to the bottom of my mouth, resulting in slurred, slow, often indistinct speech. It was a fairly mild speech impediment, but I was ashamed of it.

At school, this resulted in me retreating into silences of my own, and only being happy to participate if I could do so in writing. Anything oral led me to withdraw into an inner space. Yet I made friends, special, hand-picked friends, two now in particular: Sheila Armstrong and Margaret Foreman.

Margaret Foreman and her sister Janet lived in the house behind St Margaret's School, the house that Mrs Hunter herself had once lived in. They both had fiery red hair, and Margaret was very tall; she towered over us all. We became very close friends, and she is the only childhood friend I am still in touch with. She's now the artist Maggie Cheek.

Maggie has a memory of me being very good at art. She told me recently that she has a clear memory of me making a pop-up scene, with a story attached to it. Apparently, I called this world 'Cactus Branch Ranch' and she remembers the paper cacti all individually drawn. There were horses in the scene as well. I have no recollection at all of Cactus Branch Ranch, but I do remember my love for horses.

There were two kinds of horses in British Guiana. Most of them were bony, weary nags that plodded around town drawing dray-carts loaded with coconuts, or banana leaves or wooden boards, with red rags on the ends that stuck out beyond the long creaking carts. I felt sorry for those hacks, and their counterparts, the poor little grey donkeys with their much-smaller carts.

But the horses I revered were those elegant, well-groomed, beautiful creatures of the Mounted Branch of the police, who pranced daintily, sometimes in twos, sometimes in whole troops, as they patrolled the streets of Georgetown. They regularly clip-clopped past our house as the Mounted Branch headquarters was just around the corner. They fascinated me. The sound of clattering hooves on tarmac made my blood race and my feelings explode. I couldn't leave it alone. I had to explore.

The Mounted Branch headquarters had a training paddock, a manège, and a long low stall where all the horses were kept, some tied and some in loose-boxes. For me, this was a magnet. I'd go there almost daily and walk down the rows of boxes, stroking their noses, learning their names and talking to them. Sometimes I'd take Margaret or Sheila. Both were horsey girls, and that was the secret of our intimacy.

One day, I said to Margaret, 'Let's adopt Tessa!' Tessa was an old mare who was about to be retired. We were afraid she'd be sent to the knackers, and both of us were outraged by the idea. 'But where will we keep her?' she asked. The obvious answer was at one of our houses. 'Aunt Leila would never allow it,' I said. 'She doesn't like animals.'

'Then at my house,' said Margaret. 'We can tether her to one of the pillars and graze her every day on the parade ground in Kingston.'

Together we marched up to the sergeant in charge.

'We'll take Tessa,' I said.

'My parents are very keen!' Margaret piped up.

'Oh, really?' was the sceptical reply.

'Yes, really! You can come and talk to them!'

The sergeant must have somehow believed her – there's no telling what white people will take it into their heads to do, after all! – and came to discuss it with her dad. Mr Foreman burst out laughing, and the sergeant joined in. We couldn't understand it.

The one photo I have of my other friend, Sheila Armstrong, was taken right there at the Mounted Branch headquarters. Sheila's father was the head of Sproston's Shipping, one of the two major shipping companies in the country, and she lived at Sproston's Dock House in Lombard Street, which was – not surprisingly – right next to the docks.

This was quite a rough commercial area, with her house wedged between industrial buildings, businesses, offices and run-down houses, and it was all quite noisy and grim. To access the house, you actually had to pass through a shipbuilding area, but once you got inside the house itself was, naturally, fit for an English family – a bit of luxury tucked between its tightly-packed, run-down neighbours. It had a swimming pool, narrow and wedged between the house and its next-door neighbour's fence but a swimming pool all the same, and I spent many a sunny afternoon in it. It was there I taught myself to swim.

Even more exciting than the swimming pool was the shipyard and the dry dock. Those were our playgrounds. Sheila, Margaret and I swarmed through the noisy yard where sweaty men in singlets worked the machines; where cogs turned and metal joints were welded; where sparks flew and engines clanged as ships were repaired and built. Sometimes there'd be a ship in the dry dock, and we'd swarm over that, too. My clearest memory is of Sheila and me attempting to walk tightrope along a plank balanced over a dry dock abyss. I don't think we got very far. Nobody ever forbade us from playing in the shipyard, but perhaps someone intervened on that occasion.

Margaret has other memories of Sproston's Dock House. She recalls Sheila's house having a very big attic. She remembers wooden beams in the same memory as running along the wooden docks. We were quite convinced, she remembers, that we had the same magic powers as Supergirl. Our powers extended to solving crimes, but the only mystery we could ever find to solve was some disappearing washing.

For some reason neither of us quite understood, borrowed black macs were involved, and masks, but the idea of sleuthing in them was quickly abandoned in the tropical heat. Nevertheless, we had our comic strip fantasy, and we practised flying together across lined-up beds.

Outside of school I wore shorts, or 'long pants'. You could do so much more in those. You could venture down the gutter alleyways with your jam jars catching guppies and tadpoles, and you could climb trees and do the things boys did, and you didn't have to stay inside and play tea-party with other girls. On my feet, I wore scruffy tennis shoes without socks, or delilahs, our word for flip-flops. My feet were always dirty; Aunt Leila was constantly scrubbing them, complaining all the time.

My shining example was George from the Famous Five. George, whose real name was Georgina, and who aligned herself more to her big cousins Julian and Dick; rambunctious George, who went on adventures and caught the baddies; fearless George, who crept from her bed at night to sneak out and row her boat across to Kirrin

Island; George, with her precious dog Timmy, for whom there were no rules and no boundaries. *That* was who I wanted to be.

And there we have it: the two sides to my character. On the one hand, excruciatingly shy. On account of my speech impediment, and the embarrassment it caused, I could not speak a word to anyone I didn't know, and probably came across as rude to these people. I couldn't even let them hear my voice. Sometimes this even applied to family members. I was once in my dad's car, in the front passenger seat, chatting away merrily to him as he drove. Suddenly, a voice from the back seat piped up, and in horror I turned around to see one of my aunts sitting there. She'd been there the whole time without my noticing her, and she'd heard my voice! It was a first-class calamity; a moment of high drama for me. But nobody knew how I felt except me. I simply clammed up, and didn't speak a further word.

I became overprotective of my voice, as if it were a great secret to be kept for myself. Something private and intimate, which only very select people were allowed to hear. Feeling more confident with fictional characters than with real people, I would retreat into a book and be lost to the world for hours, complete unto myself, silent and absorbed. I already had a tendency to introversion, but my voice became a further reason to withdraw into myself, keeping my thoughts and reflections secret.

Yet at the very same time I craved adventure, and that was my other side, the other half of my personality. I was practically fearless as long as I didn't have to talk; always willing and ready for the next big challenge, whether it was tightrope walking over an abyss, or – if only in my dreams – galloping bareback over a prairie on a wild pony, mane and tail flying. New trials lured me. I didn't mind being alone, anywhere, and feared nothing; if you'd invited me along to plunge through the Amazon jungle, I'd have been right there in a shot – and I actually did do this, years later.

But right now, the only jungle I could explore was my own backyard, with its trees, ants, lizards, birds, caterpillars, butterflies, tadpoles and frogs. I watched these little creatures, observed them silently, and wondered about the nature of their inner being. Did they know they were alive? Did they think? Did they feel themselves as clearly as I did? Did they have an I, a Me? Did they… just know? These were the questions that plagued me, the reason for my introversion. I had a strong need to understand, to probe deeper, ever deeper, into my own sense of just *being*.

There was a dual me. A child with two distinct sides, each the opposite of the other. I turned inward, to the exclusion of the outer world, shutting it out completely and happy in my own silences, but yet was ready at a moment's notice to tightrope-walk through the outer world, without a safety net, reckless and fearless, throwing myself at an uncaring and sometimes dangerous reality.

I was shy, silent, never speaking to adults except ones I knew well, locked away in my own being, happy in the silence. I was withdrawn when faced with strangers, clamming up, not speaking a word, so that they'd think me dumb and dull. And yet I was perfectly capable, when the time came, of flying across the ocean to a new continent, a new world filled with perfect strangers. I craved the 'other'. Other places, other experiences; a life that took me away from the familiar and into unknown situations, with people different from me in every way.

What people couldn't see was the active, vibrant processing of it all within me. All I was doing was trying to figure it all out. Figure *them* all out, and understand the world, all on my own.

Chapter Twenty-Two

The Sea, the Sea

About the time I turned seven, Mum was off again. She'd been offered a good job with the West Indies Federation, the short-lived political union of a collection of West Indian nations established in January 1958. I suppose Mum could have, and would have, taken me with her; I could have gone to school in Port-of-Spain. But I was happy and thriving at St Margaret's, well cared for at home in Lamaha Street, and Daddy would have raised objections. So why disrupt my life? Nothing really changed because Aunt Leila continued in her role *in loco parentis.* So I stayed behind, showered Mum with letters written at my little blue desk, and visited her when I could.

I went to stay with her in Port-of-Spain in all the school holidays. The first time, she came to collect me, which meant her flying out to Guyana alone and back to Port-of-Spain with me. If she did the reverse at the end of the holidays, there would be more expenses and disruptions, so instead, she sent me home alone.

I was the first child to fly all by myself on a BWIA (British West Indian Airlines, now Caribbean Airlines) plane: a new thing for the region. I even made the newspapers: *Child Flies Alone on BWIA!* A photo of the groundbreaking news was published in all the papers, of me walking across the tarmac to the arrivals hall, hand in hand with a stewardess. After that, the hour's flight alone to visit Mum became routine. I felt all grown-up and independent.

In Port-of-Spain Mum lived with her brother, my Uncle Percy. Uncle Percy was married to Aunt Rita, the Trinidadian woman of Indian background who had minded me as a baby. They had four children, Reggie, Algy, Gale and Gregory, with Cousin Algy being exactly my age. Aunt Rita became one in a string of mothers I revered, looking up to her as the kind of mother I wanted for myself, with the family I wished I had.

Aunt Rita's home was filled with love and good cheer. She was one of those warm-hearted, motherly women who have a natural rapport with children, and I couldn't help but compare Mum unfavourably with her. She was an excellent cook, and though I was still a picky eater, I loved being a part of a 'real' family, at whose heart was a mother who cooked for and fed her children and was always there for them when they came home from school, who you could confide everything to, pour out all your questions and troubles and find answers and options. A disgraceful wish, perhaps, for the daughter of my country's leading feminist, but there it was. Of course, I never told Mum. I'd long been in the habit of knowing which thoughts and feelings I should keep to myself, out of tact, politeness or avoidance of conflict.

Perhaps I should have been more outspoken from the start, more forthright. But that was just the way I was. I shunned conflict. I loved silence and solitude, and so felt no need to disrupt others with my own, contrary, opinions on matters. Mum respected that. She never saw my reticence as a problem and never tried to break it. She didn't think, as I suspect a twenty-first-century parent would, that I needed to 'come out of my shell'. She left me the way I was and took all her leads from me; if I wanted to talk, she listened, and we'd have a conversation, but if I didn't, she wouldn't force me. That was her strength, but also her weakness. I was a child who, if I had a question or a problem, did not ask adults for help but tried to solve it by myself, within myself.

Uncle Percy and Mum were very close. I looked up to him in my shy and silent way, not least because I was so impressed by his job. Uncle Percy was Port-of-Spain's deputy chief fire officer, and his house – still standing – was right next door to the fire station on Wrightson Road. Sometimes, in the middle of the night, the fire alarm would blare out, a clanging sound that would rouse me out of sleep with my heart racing, and the lights at the fire station would flare on, and the fire engines would all race off, sirens screaming.

Every day Mummy took me to work with her. She worked in a tall building in the middle of Port-of-Spain called Federal House. It was one of the tallest buildings in the city, and she worked on the top floor, with a direct view of the sea. On a clear day you could see the coastline of Venezuela.

Meanwhile, on the home front, I played with the boys, Algy and Reggie. Gale was a bit too young for me, and Gregory just a baby, but I liked the rough and tumble of boyish games. Yet I never spoke to them; they were of that class of humans not allowed to hear my voice. I played by simply tagging along. And I almost never ate Aunt Rita's delicious meals. It was still drumsticks for me, which was most frustrating for Mum.

'You know what?' she said one day. 'Let's go to a restaurant for lunch!'

And so she took me to a posh, atmospheric Port-of-Spain restaurant with soft lights and even softer music. I ate a complete meal of lamb chops. Mum, delighted, went around telling everyone afterwards: *She's eaten a full meal! She likes lamb!* But it never happened again, as Mum couldn't really afford fancy restaurant meals. But if she could have, she would have. She was that kind of mother; whatever I wanted, she'd give and give. I didn't want much in the way of food. I did develop a liking for peanut punch, and that became my midday snack during her work hours.

The thing was, what I really wanted was *her*, and here in Port-of-Spain I had a lot more of her than back home in BG. What was special about living in Port-of-Spain was that Mummy had her job, and that was it. She did not feel the need to change Trinidadian society; it wasn't her home, wasn't her nation, wasn't her duty. She had time for me, after work, and on the weekends. We did things together, things we'd never do back home in BG. I had her full attention. I loved Trinidad. I often wished it were my real home, that *this* was where we lived, *together*. A family of two.

I wished that Mummy and I could settle there, and we could go to the beach each weekend. It was there that I fell in love with the Caribbean Sea. Mummy and I would sometimes drive out to Maracas Bay or other local beaches. I'd be in a state of higher and higher excitement the closer we got to the sea and, as the first glimpse of the sparkling blue appeared, we'd chant together: *I see the sea! I see the sea!* Then another hill would appear, another corner, and the sea would disappear, only to pop into sight again a few minutes later: *I see the sea!*

I was an easy child for a parent to take to work. I did not need entertainment; a book was all I wanted. Mum could park me on the floor next to the air-conditioning unit, where I'd sit cross-legged, absorbed in my book for hours on end. But I didn't only read, I also thought things over. I thought a lot. I'd sit, gazing into the distance, trying to figure it all out. You know: the secrets of life, the enigmas philosophers from the beginning of time have sought to puzzle out. They became, for me, urgent puzzles.

Who am I? Where do I come from? What is a feeling? What is the feeling of being me? Does everyone else have the same feeling of me-ness, as I do? What makes people different? Why do they differ? What is a thought? Where does it come from? Why do I think? What would happen if I stopped thinking? Can I even stop thinking? What is in the space between thoughts? Is it just nothingness?

I tried, I really did, to stop thinking. To stop thoughts. But I couldn't, and I gave up. Nevertheless, these questions were to rear their heads later in my life, and became central to the journey I was later to set off on. As a seven-year-old child, I already had the makings of a philosopher. But then came an unforgettable trip to the other side of the island.

One day a friend invited us on a day trip across the island to a place called Blanchisseuse. It was a trip to see a waterfall, and involved hiking through the forest to find it. That was fun.

But the beach at Blanchisseuse was better. It was there, sitting on that beach, gazing out at the horizon, that I had the first glimpse of the mystery of myself, and found many of my questions answered. A feeling overwhelmed me, a feeling beyond the ordinary. In fact it was more than just a feeling: it was an experience, engulfing my entire consciousness. I was enfolded by an ocean of utter bliss, a happiness far beyond anything I had ever experienced in my life before. A sense of absolute completeness, wholeness, in which nothing at all was missing; a sense of perfection far beyond thought, which seemed to have dissolved entirely. It could not be put into words but it was real, so real, realer than my everyday sense of me-ness, as if my little personality was but a small bubble, whose membrane was suddenly broken, to merge 'me' into this vast ocean of sheer beauty. And all those questions, all the mysteries I'd contemplated sitting next to that air conditioner hugging my knees at Federal House: they were all answered in one stroke, in one second.

There is no logical, rational answer to those questions. It was the Blanchisseuse experience that gave me all the answers I needed, every single one, while trying to work out the Secret of Life. Here at Blanchisseuse, all doubts were swept away. Words remained inadequate, arguments dissolved into clear light. The word Blanchisseuse became, ever after, an encapsulation of that experience, bringing back the memory.

I loved Trinidad so much that, back home, I began to tell porky-pies. I would tell people I was actually Trinidadian, that I was born there and lived there. Travelling back and forth between here and there was the beginning of my yearning for far-off shores.

Occasionally, Mum and I went on holiday to other Caribbean Islands. Once we went to Barbados, once to St Lucia, once to Tobago, the last on a ferry from Port-of-Spain, a passenger boat called the *Scarlet Ibis*. I was violently seasick on that vessel. We returned on the *Bird of Paradise*, and again I was violently seasick. But Tobago was unbelievably gorgeous, as were all of the islands and the Caribbean Sea itself.

Mum took me to a hotel called the Blue Waters Beach Hotel in St Lucia. I loved it. I loved the transparent turquoise sea and the wide beaches of soft sand. When I returned to Guyana – straight from St Lucia – and Aunt Leila combed out my hair, she laughed. 'I know what colour the sand was! Yellow!' she said, and it was true. Our sand in BG was greyish-brown, the ocean water uninvitingly, boringly, opaquely brown. BG's Atlantic waters were actually Amazon waters, from the mouth of that great river drifting northwards up the coast. It's why the Caribbean islanders gave us the disparaging name *mudheads*.

Guyana would never be a mass-tourism country, never a destination for holidaymakers who wanted a picture-postcard beach with transparent turquoise waters and white sandy shores. For the very first time, a traitorous sting nipped at me. I wanted to leave. Find a better place. It was the beginning of a vague restlessness as I began to compare and contrast, to yearn for far-off places, new worlds to discover. The word I'm looking for is a German word with the literal meaning 'distance pain': *Fernweh*. It's the opposite of homesickness, and there's no English equivalent. I was infected with *Fernweh* from a ridiculously young age. It's a disease that when it grips you takes you in its jaws and never lets you go. A most disloyal, unpatriotic disease. I caught it early. Those trips to Trinidad and the islands were just the start of it.

Back then, I envied all those who left BG. Once, I went to bid farewell to my Uncle Patrick's family: his wife, Zena, and my cousins, Roderick and Gillian. I was allowed to accompany them on board the ship. Oh, how I envied them! The very smell of that vessel, the steep staircases, the narrow corridors smelling of salt and paint and shiply things, the little cabin with the porthole, the lifeboats, the crew, the hustle and bustle of passengers embarking, hoisting their luggage here and there, children crying, people hugging and weeping their goodbyes. My heart quickened and a seed was sown. I, too, would one day sail away.

Or I would fly away; and, a couple of years later, I did. My younger cousins Rod and Gillian, by now at home in London, would point to the sky whenever a plane passed overhead and say, 'Look! It's Sharon!' because I had come grandly, by air.

Flying away was something of an event in those days. We made it an event. Whenever a family member flew out of Atkinson Field, the airport an hour's drive inland from Georgetown, it was only good manners to drive up to say goodbye. The entire family, dressed in their Sunday best, would gather for a last drink and a last meal in the departure area of the Base, as we called the airport. After that, those who were left behind would go up to the viewing balcony to wave goodbye, watch their loved ones walk across the tarmac and disappear into those enormous birds of metal; and, in my case, long for my own take-off.

And yet, trips to the Base did not fill me with the same wistful longing as did ocean-bound ships. I was used to flying; to me it meant holiday-time, to join Mum in Port-of-Spain. It was the sea, the glorious, boundless sea, the faraway horizon, that called, and always had.

Chapter Twenty-Three

Bad Break

It happened when I was about nine, while visiting friends in Kingston. We were playing in the Bottom House. The boys were climbing up on a pile of planks, leaping to catch one of the rafters, swinging a few times, then jumping to the ground. I tried to copy them, leapt for the rafter, missed, and fell to the concrete. It was curiously painless at the time, but it looked and felt odd. There I sat, holding up my hand and staring at it: 'My hand! I think it's broken!'

Someone, probably the friends' parents, drove me to the hospital, where I was soon joined by Dad. A bone between thumb and forefinger was broken, they told us. They put me under anaesthetic and set it. Waking up from the anaesthetic, I was convinced I heard voices – nurses or doctors – saying 'She almost died!' I never told anyone, but it was my conviction. Who knows?

They put me in a bed in a huge ward full of children. To me, it seemed like there were a hundred, most of them crying or screaming, day and night, and a couple of them running about too. Dad came to visit every day. He tried to get me relocated to a quieter ward with fewer children, but no luck. I had to stick it out.

In the bed next to me was a little Amerindian boy called Charlie, an orphan who lived in St Anne's orphanage. Charlie had polio and had very thin, very bowed legs. He couldn't walk without callipers, but he hated using them, so he lay in bed most of the time. Apparently, he had spent most of his life so far in hospital and had never been to the cinema. All of this Dad found out through chatting with him. Charlie was a year or two younger than me.

'How would you like to go with us to see a film?' Dad asked him one day. Charlie's eyes lit up. 'Yes!' he cried.

'I'll have to ask the nurses,' said Dad, and he did. He must have got permission because a few days after I was discharged, Daddy came back to the hospital, picked up Charlie, carried him to our car and into the Metropole, where the three of us laughed ourselves silly over a Jerry Lewis film.

The Charlie story is so typical of Dad. Like Mum, he was a people person, with a big heart for the underdog, the poor and needy. Both instilled in me the sense that our first duty was to those less fortunate than ourselves, a need to help when and where we could. What Mum and Dad had in common was a genuine caring for the disadvantaged and oppressed, a genuine distrust and dislike of those who used their power for their own selfish ambition, and a willingness to engage. Both cared deeply about society's ills and dedicated their lives to making it better in any way they could. 'Power corrupts; absolute power corrupts absolutely!' was one of the maxims Dad drummed into me, as well as 'the love of money is the root of all evil'. Mum was distrustful of monopolies all her life; that was one of the reasons why she was later to found the Guyana Consumers Association, to protect the people and let them know their rights. Neither were impressed by riches and both deemed personal integrity to be the higher virtue. Neither could ever be bought or lured away from their principles. Both did their best to walk their talk.

Mum did so by throwing herself into action, generating new guilds and groups to bring about change. Dad did so through established political avenues. Like Uncle Rory, he found a political home in Marxism and the PPP, the People's Progressive Party. Later, Mum told me it was one of the reasons she divorced him: she could not align with that, or any, ideology.

But for Dad, his politics was one of the two columns on which he rested, the other being Family, with a capital F. By this time, Dad had remarried, to a pretty young woman named Faye whom he had courted with touching persistence, and won. She was the perfect wife for him, and by now they'd had two sons, Nigel and Gary, and would go on to have two more. Theirs was a solid marriage that lasted over forty years, until his death parted them.

Mum, on the other hand, was never to remarry and never to date. She was good enough for herself. But how I hated having a single mother calling herself Miss Cox, having to fend off accusations of being a bastard – a scandalous thing! – and being asked why my name was different from hers; and why I lived with my granny and not with my parents. I felt ashamed, and mumbled replies, but I was certain I was the talk of the town, being whispered about behind my back. All untrue, of course! People had more salty items of gossip to talk about than prim and proper Eileen Cox. Yet still I longed for normality. Simultaneously, there grew in me a need to defend my parents, my mother, myself. I wanted to find the strength to fight back, find in myself an assurance that it wasn't true. I wasn't inferior – neither my skin, nor my hair, nor my mother who was a Miss, nor my father who didn't live at home, nor anything in the world made me subordinate.

Mum being away in Port-of-Spain meant that I got to spend more time with Dad, who now lived in a downstairs flat at the Crown Street house with his growing family. I had to share him with his wife and the boys, but I'd always enjoyed family life; I had a good rapport with Faye and adored the two little ones, just as I adored all helpless little living things. But best of all was when I had Dad all to myself.

It was around this time, in 1960, that British Guiana carried out a census. Dad worked as a census taker, which meant going from house to house and personally counting the people in each household. It took place during the long school holidays, and before jetting off to Port-of-Spain I stayed with him for a while. It was a perfect, almost idyllic time, as good as a beach holiday; just us two, together. He'd take me with him on long drives up the East Coast Demerara in his green Ford Prefect. He'd park outside the higgledy-piggledy villages and go into the houses and count the people and chat with them, and I went with him, waiting while he interviewed them. East Indian mothers would pinch my cheeks and say, 'Ow, *beti*! What a sweet little girl!' And I'd play with their dogs, feed their chickens, play with their children, eat the bananas and mangoes and genips they offered me, or simply sit in the shade of a tree or on the stairs and read a book until Dad had finished counting the people and we moved on to the next house.

The East Coast Demerara has a serenity to it, a sense of the endlessness of time and space with the flatness of the coast merging with the watery plane of the ocean beyond the Sea Wall, reaching out to the horizon. We'd see women knee-deep and bent double in the emerald-green rice fields, or fishermen on the muddy beaches hauling in their catch of the day. We'd drive past coconut groves and sugar-cane fields, quaint villages with tiny wooden houses balanced precariously on tall thin stilts, like oversized cranes that could topple at any moment. Dogs, cows and chickens sprinkled between the fields and the houses. Coconut palms waving against the brilliant blue sky, and mango, banana and papaya trees. The cool Atlantic breeze sweeping between the trees and the houses. There's a timelessness about it all. A changelessness. An unhurried sense of *yes, this is it. This is what life is about.* No hurry, no haste, no great goal to achieve, no great success to wrangle from life, just being. Being, here and now. Not being this or being that. Being, without further attributes.

And yet. Nothing could cure the gnawing restlessness within me, the need to move on, to evolve, explore, change, have adventures, discover new worlds, discover myself. And so, instead of just *Being,* I *became.* I became Jo.

Chapter Twenty-Four

The Making of Jo

I wanted to be a boy. Boys, obviously, had more fun. They were allowed to have adventures, explore, do exciting and even dangerous things. They didn't have to wear pink frothy dresses and dance cutely at parties and sit around in galleries with old ladies in the evening. How I loathed that stupid old rhyme:

> *What are little girls made of?*
> *What are little girls made of?*
> *Sugar and spice and everything nice;*
> *That's what little girls are made of.*
> *What are little boys made of?*
> *What are little boys made of?*
> *Sticks and snails and puppy-dog tails;*
> *That's what little boys are made of.*

I most definitely slotted into the second part of that rhyme, not the first. It was obvious that I was just like George of the Famous Five.

Indulgent as ever, Mum did as I asked – or 'demanded' is perhaps a more apt word. When she came home for the holidays the Christmas I turned nine, she officially added the middle name Josephine to my birth certificate. Aunt Leila took me to a hairdresser friend of hers, who cut my hair short. My beautiful, shoulder-long mass of curls was cut away in a symbolic act of rebellion: rebellion against the rules and structures placed on me as a girl; rebellion against all the dolls and frilly dresses and ribbons I was supposed to wear. It was an initiation into a different world, one in which I could claim freedom. From that day on I was officially a boy, called Jo by everyone, proud and free.

From there it was only a heartbeat to the next overwhelming desire. I began to bombard Mum, still in Port-of-Spain, with begging letters.

I was nine when I started my completely unrealistic pestering of Mum to send me to an English boarding-school. I'd read the books: Malory Towers, St Clare's, The Naughtiest Girl in the School. Dormitories, draconian French mistresses, midnight feasts, pranks, punishments, detentions, rules all day long, and endless fun.

I already knew, deep inside, what would await me: a scaffolding for the limp vine of my growing personality. A rudder to help me through the stormy ocean of life. Hopelessly confused by all the freedoms and choices offered to me, I instinctively felt the need for clearly defined boundaries and a circumscribed concept for navigating the complexities of life. I needed clear ethical guidance to replace the very fuzzy and rather lame 'do what you want as long as you don't hurt anybody' principles presented by my mother. Perhaps I instinctively felt that just doing what I wanted made me weak, unable to withstand the external demands life presented me with. I *wanted* rules and guidelines. I *demanded* them.

At the same time, my nibbling *Fernweh* grew stronger. I loved travelling. I loved visiting other countries, other shores. I still had those vague memories of England, from our family visit when I was three. Back and forth between Georgetown and Port-of-Spain, holidays in Barbados, St Lucia, Tobago; each new place I visited expanded my awareness, made me in an internal sense bigger, wider, better. I wanted more.

Books took me to far-off places, too. The Bobbsey Twins and Nancy Drew and the Hardy Boys took me to America. A book about a girl called Hilda who rode horses took me to Australia. But thanks to Enid Blyton, my soul settled in England. I could almost taste those strawberries with lashings of cream. I smelled the flowers, galloped on ponies over green hills, and with all my lovely English friends I played tricks on the French mistress, hid stashes of food in preparation for a midnight feast, and simply had loads and loads of jolly times.

Those books about St Clare's and Malory Towers, girls' boarding schools in that faraway green and pleasant land, a land with a queen who rode a horse on the cinema screen before every film while the British national anthem played and the whole audience rose to their feet in respect: that was the England I longed for. Most of all, I longed for horses. Ponies. Those lovely stomping, snorting mares and geldings at the Mounted Branch no longer satisfied me. I wanted more, much more. I wanted to ride.

And so I began to pester Mum. *Please, please, please: send me to boarding school in England!*

How was I to know, at the age of nine, that on her mid-level employee's salary at Federal House she could not possibly afford boarding school fees, or to maintain me in England? That she wasn't some wealthy senior executive of a prosperous corporation, who could easily educate her children at a posh English public school across the ocean? That she had not inherited a fortune? And that Dad, as a mid-level civil servant, also could not possibly afford to give me an English boarding-school education?

But an English education for her only daughter! It must have lit a spark in Mum's mind and she decided it was the right thing to do. Education was the key to a better life, and an English education – well, it was the best in the world, wasn't it? Mum had high ambitions for me. I'd follow in her brilliant footsteps and do even better, go one step further, because I'd have an English education.

Maybe I'd go on to Oxford, or Cambridge. Certainly, university, which was so rare for Guianese women of the era. Maybe I'd be a top lawyer, or a doctor, and the sure path along that route would undoubtedly start at a good English school. And so she agreed to send me.

At the time I never questioned how she could afford it. I never asked. Children don't ask these things. As long as your parents aren't scrimping and scrounging to make ends meet – and mine weren't – we truly believe that money falls like manna into our parents' pockets. It's what Mum told me again and again later on: *You think money grows on trees!* I did indeed think that I could have whatever I wanted, and right now, it was a new life in England, with an expensive school combined with riding lessons and ponies. I had none of her frugal nature. I took it all for granted.

It was only much later that I discovered exactly how she managed to pay the considerable school fees and travel and maintenance costs. In 1961, the year I turned ten, the West Indies Federation was dissolved, and all the employees had to be compensated. Mum was given the choice between a pension for life or a lump sum to be paid immediately. Not knowing how long she would live, she chose the lump sum. The money all went into a sterling account at Lombard Bank – later to become the National Westminster Bank, better known as NatWest – and was spent almost entirely on my education and the requisites for such.

As efficient as ever, Mum went about organising my new life. First, we had to choose the school. As if by magic – I never asked where she got it from – a big fat book fell into our hands, listing all the boarding schools in England, Scotland and Wales. She gave it to me, giving me permission to peruse it carefully and pick my school. I scoured the listings. They each had photos of the school and a description beneath the photo of what it offered. But I was looking for one thing only: horses. *Did they offer riding as an extra-curricular option?* That was all that mattered to me.

I looked up from the book, my finger on the page.

'This one, Mum! This school!'

She took the book from me. 'Harrogate Ladies' College?'

I nodded. 'Yes! They have riding, and ponies!'

'Hmmm. Let me read.' She read through the entry, and looked up. 'It seems like a good school. If that's the one you want...'

I nodded vigorously. 'That's the one.'

It wasn't just the riding and the ponies; I liked the look of the building, too. It seemed like a nice place. Harrogate – where was that? Neither of us knew what kind of a town it was – posh, I learned later – and we didn't know where in England it was, or how far it was from London – many hours away, again as I learned later on – as we had no map. We didn't know that we weren't nearly posh enough for Harrogate. That my background was all wrong. That I'd stick out like a sore thumb in that school. We didn't know if it was a good school, sending its graduates on to Oxford and Cambridge, or a failing one. None of that mattered. I had made my decision, and that was my future school. Where I'd finally learn to ride.

Mum launched herself into action. Airmail letters flew back and forth across the Atlantic. I had to sit two examinations, the school clerk told her, in arithmetic and English. The exam papers would be sent from the school and I would sit them under the watchful eye of Mrs Hunter, who would return them to Harrogate. I sat the exams and did my best. Mum was still working in Port-of-Spain at this time, but a few weeks later she sent me a telegram:

Examination successful school September.

I was ecstatic.

Unknown to me, floating as I was in my bubble of delight, Mum was busying herself with all the practicalities. There were flights to book, and plans for my holidays to be organised. Where would

I go? I couldn't possibly come home for all the holidays; a foster home had to be found. Once again, Mum managed to access all the necessary information, and as ever, I was allowed to choose.

I made my choice of foster-family along the same criteria I had used for choosing the school: ponies. As a side dish, there'd be a foster-mother or foster-parents, but ponies were the most important thing. Letters from various foster-family applicants poured in. I scrutinised them, and made my choice: Mrs Joan Williamson, a single, middle-aged woman who ran a riding school in Cumberland. Perfect! Letters flew back and forth between Mrs Williamson and Mum, and all was arranged.

Originally, Mum had planned to fly out with me to England in September and accompany me to the school in Yorkshire, but for some reason she couldn't. Possibly she couldn't afford a second return flight. Or maybe she couldn't get leave.

She broke the sad news to me. 'Darling, I can't come with you! You'll have to fly over on your own. Do you think you can manage that?'

I cried, a thing I seldom did. It was a scary thought, flying all the way to England by myself. I had so looked forward to flying out with Mum. I'd vividly imagined her bringing me to school, all the other girls arriving with their parents, showing Mum my new dorm, meeting the headmistress with her. But Mum made it clear that it just wasn't possible at this time.

'I'll come and visit you as soon as I can!' she promised, and I had to make do with that. It was a huge disappointment. 'You're a big girl now,' Mum said. 'Almost ten!'

But *no*, I thought. I was a *boy!* Boys are brave. Boys don't cry if their mummy can't fly with them across the ocean. Remember George, of the Famous Five. *She* wouldn't cry!

With that inspiration, I quickly pulled myself together. If I could fly to Trinidad alone, I could fly to England. It was simply a new adventure. In September I'd turn ten. I *could* and I *would* do it! In no time at all I was enrolled at Oakdale School, the prep school for Harrogate Ladies' College, and I was to fly out, all on my own, the day before the autumn term began.

Once again, Mum had to arrange it all, with letters flying back and forth across the Atlantic. Plans had to be made for me to fly as an unaccompanied minor to London, to be picked up there by someone. I had relatives in London at the time, two uncles, Uncle Patrick with a young family and Uncle Donald with a wife and no children, but for some reason Mum chose to go it alone. She contacted a service called Universal Aunts. How did she even get to hear about this service? It's a mystery, but she did it; I suspect there must have been helpful staff at the British Consulate.

Universal Aunts had been founded by a lady called Gertrude Maclean in 1921, and had the aim of caring for children whose parents lived overseas. With brothers and sisters scattered all over the British Commonwealth, Aunt Gertrude took over the role of looking after her nephews and nieces who were sent back to school in Britain. According to their website today, with the end of the First World War, Gertrude's brothers and sisters came home. She bemoaned the passing of her usefulness, until an elderly uncle suggested, 'Why not do for others what you have been doing for your own family?' Gertrude's reply was instantaneous: 'And be a Universal Aunt.'

Mum went about arranging my arrival in London and dispatch to Harrogate with her customary efficiency. I had to be picked up at Heathrow, spend the night at a stranger's home, and then be taken to King's Cross the following day to meet a group of pupils and a mistress also heading to Harrogate.

To make it all much more exciting, it was now my turn to write letters. I received a blue airmail form, which consisted of a sheet of light paper folded and sealed to form a letter with an integrated postage stamp, addressed not to Mummy, but to me, in childish handwriting. It was from a girl my age, called Carole.

She wrote,

> *I am your school mother, and we can be pen-pals until you*
> *come to school. And I will show you around and explain*
> *everything to you. I hope we can be friends.*

What a delightful letter! I was more than excited and wrote back immediately. From then until my departure in September, Carole and I wrote letters to each other, and she told me a little of what I was to expect: that we would share a dormitory, and what the teachers were like, and the headmistress. 'Her name is Miss Killingley,' Carole wrote, 'but we call her Killer. She's really scary.'

Part Three

England 1961–63

First Term at Oakdale School

Chapter Twenty-Five

King's Cross to Harrogate

Dear Mum,

I arrived safely in London. The Universal Aunt picked me up at the airport. Her name is Miss Sutcliffe. She has a little dog, a Pekinese. She lives in a big building in London but she doesn't live in the whole building, just a few rooms in the middle of it. It's very small and London is very big.

The next day she took me to the station and put me on the train. I am now at Oakdale. It is a castle! A real castle!

It is Sunday today and we have to write letters home on Sunday. I don't miss you very much because I don't have time.

I am in a dorm with my school mother. Her name is pronounced Carol, like normal, not Ca-role.

Love, Jo

'Hello! You must be Miss Sutcliffe. This is Jo.' The BOAC stewardess smiled brightly at the rather portly middle-aged woman at the airline's desk. Miss Sutcliffe, accepting deliverance of the precious package – me – held out her hand and smiled.

'Hello, Jo. I'm Miss Sutcliffe. I hope you had a nice flight.'

I nodded and shook the proffered hand – that is, I put my limp little hand into the big open one and let it be squeezed. Shaking hands was not really a thing we did in BG. Overcome by another wave of shyness, I tried to smile back. I could not speak a word.

'Where's your luggage, then?' she continued.

'She didn't bring any. There's just this small bag.' The stewardess handed over the overnight bag I'd brought with me.

'That's all? It's not much, is it? Oh well. A parcel has arrived with your school uniform, Jo. It's all you'll need for the time being.'

We took a bus to her flat, which was somewhere in central London. It was a small flat, rather crowded with furniture. She had a small lapdog that yapped at me. I crouched down and tried to make friends with it. I felt more at home with the dog than with Miss Sutcliffe, but that was typical. To her credit, Miss Sutcliffe was friendly enough and did try to make conversation, but my lips were sealed. My shyness was overpowering. I could not speak a word.

Nothing exemplifies my dual personality more than my arrival in London, shortly before my tenth birthday; on the one hand paralysed by shyness, unable to speak a word, on the other fearless, compliant, ready to plunge into new situations with new people without turning a hair. I was ready. The adventure had begun. Here I was, in London!

There was indeed a package waiting for me, containing those items of my new uniform I'd need for the trip to Yorkshire the following day. This was the reason I'd brought so little with me: my BG clothes would be absolutely useless in England, especially at this time of year, early September. For the next couple of months, all I'd need was my new school uniform.

Once again, Mum's meticulous cross-Atlantic organisational skills stood me in good stead. It was all there, everything I'd need. I wouldn't even need my old knickers, because even knickers were regulation: dark green, somewhat baggy serge bloomers, and white cotton knicker-linings. Harrogate Ladies' College, and by extension

Oakdale Prep School, had its own uniform outfitters, a Glasgow company called R.W. Forsyth. Mum had ordered the entire collection for me, down to socks, shoes and handkerchiefs, as well as knickers, to be delivered to the school in a trunk.

But she had also arranged for a set of travelling clothes to be sent to Miss Sutcliffe in London so that I would arrive at school appropriately attired. This meant a dark-green serge dress with a removable cream collar bearing the Oakdale symbol – a green three-leaved clover – as well as a green cardigan, green winter coat, green velour hat, knee-length socks, and 'walking shoes', which were brown lace-ups. All this was waiting for me at Miss Sutcliffe's, ready for the morrow when off I'd go into the great unknown.

Before we left the flat the next morning I looked at myself in the full-length mirror. How very smart I looked! How very different from the St Margaret's schoolgirl I'd once been, with my green-and-white-checked summer dress! A proper English schoolgirl! Apart from the colour of my skin.

At King's Cross, Miss Sutcliffe delivered me into the hands of the schoolmistress who would be accompanying me and a group of my co-pupils to school – again, all pre-arranged via letter by Mum. How many letters must have flown back and forth across the ocean for all this to be organised! There were about five girls around my age who'd be travelling together with this mistress, and some of them already knew each other: another cause for debilitating shyness.

Once ensconced in our compartment, the chatter began. Each girl introduced herself, and in the flurry of 'I'm so-and-so and I'm from so-and-so' at last I was able to loosen my tongue. 'Where's that?' someone said when I mentioned British Guiana, and I managed to say 'South America.' But I was already trying to process something quite astonishing.

One of the girls had introduced herself as Angela. 'I'm from Africa!' she'd added. 'Uganda!'

Africa! No, it couldn't be! I'd had geography lessons, of course, and learned about a boy called Bombo who lived in Africa. That's how we learned geography; we were introduced to a girl or a boy from a faraway country and we learned about his or her life and what it was like over there. There'd been a Norwegian girl and a French boy and an Eskimo, the word we then used for Inuits, and an Argentinian, Pedro. And Bombo, who was Black and who lived in a village with his parents. Of course, in BG Black people were known as Africans, and we had learned that they'd been brought to the Americas and the Caribbean as slaves. That was common knowledge. And somehow, I'd come to the conclusion that all Africans were Black and lived in basic villages. So to meet this white-skinned girl who'd be my schoolmate gaily declaring that she was 'from Africa' was absolutely jaw-dropping. I managed, though, to contain my surprise. I had so much to learn, and not just school lessons.

The train journey from London to Harrogate lasted many hours, a time in which I slowly and gradually lost some of my inhibitions and relaxed into the little group of boisterous girls. This was all going to be fine. Angela and all the others seemed perfectly nice.

Arriving at Harrogate station, we were all ushered into a taxi that was to take us to school. After a short drive, the taxi turned off the road into a downward-sloping wooded drive. And as the school came into view my jaw dropped for the second time that day. I may even have gasped aloud.

Oakdale School was a castle. A real, genuine, original, magnificent English castle. The kind of castle you'd read about in books, the kind of castle you'd written stories about. Castles with secret staircases and forbidden towers and moving panels released by hidden springs. Castles with turrets where prisoners could be kept and mysterious passageways to be explored, and somewhere, most certainly, a buried treasure secreted in the woods surrounding it. Castles with cryptic messages carved into the stone walls, and maybe even a skeleton in the dusty attic or the gloomy cellar, and your task was to find out whose it was. It was a vision from a fairy tale.

There it stood. This magnificent building nestled into a breathtakingly beautiful dale, the kind of place where I just knew all my dreams would be realised, and all my fantasies let loose. My new home.

Oakdale School, Harrogate; now sadly demolished

But this was no time for dreaming, no time to be inventing the wonderful stories that could all spring to mind. Bustled out of the taxi, I was soon part of a chaotic horde of chattering, screaming, excited girls, all dressed just like me, all scrambling to meet their old friends or make new ones and find their bearings for the fresh new term. I, however, silent and once more overcome by shyness, was ushered into the dark and imposing front hall and straight into Miss Killingley's presence. This was the dreaded Killer Carole had warned me about.

Killer wore the kind of smart skirt suit middle-aged ladies of the time were wont to wear: close-fitting around the hips, just covering the knees. She favoured the colour pale blue, I recall, and her hair was close-cropped, white and arranged in stiff curls. To me she seemed ancient, and absolutely terrifying. Yet she welcomed me in a somewhat un-murderous manner and before I knew it, I was being escorted by someone-or-other to what was to be my dormitory, where I was to meet my school mother, Carole, as well as my other dorm-mates.

The first thing I learned about Carole was that her name was not Car-OLE, as I'd mentally pronounced it up to now, never having seen Carol written with an e before this. The e was silent and did not alter the pronunciation. The second thing I learned about Carole was what her hair looked like: short, blonde, and very curly; a veritable mop of curls.

Carole was friendly and right away, took me under her wing. We were in a dorm called Upper Seven, which meant it had seven beds, in which slept seven girls. My bed was right next to Carole's, and beside it was my trunk with all my new things in it. A matron came bustling in. Her name was Miss Almond and she soon took charge of me and all the other New Girls.

'We call her Mummy Almond,' Carole whispered, and it was easy to see why.

'Come on, girls, unpack your trunks, fold your knickers nicely and put them away tidily in your drawers! Chop, chop, no chattering, now!'

She was not the kind of mummy I was used to, but perhaps the kind I needed: one who said what had to be done and made sure I did it. We had to unpack our trunks as quickly as possible, putting all our clothes into our appointed dressing tables and wardrobes, pyjamas under the pillows and dressing gowns on their appropriate hooks. It was all there in the trunk, down to the last hanky: everything brand new and smelling of Glasgow. Not only did it contain my uniform and shoes (three kinds: walking, house and game-shoes, plus wellingtons and slippers) but pyjamas, towels, and a pretty paisley eiderdown, with every single item efficiently labelled with my name, Jo Westmaas, on red Cash's Name Tapes neatly sewn on.

Everything packed away, we were herded to the main school for a flurry of activities: a welcome assembly in the gym including a hymn, Bible reading and prayers, supper, a bit of free time. The rest of the day and evening passed in a whirlwind of chatter and utter bewilderment and *too many girls* with *too many names*: how would I ever get used to this place?

And then it was time for sleep: changing into pyjamas, waiting my turn to wash in the communal bathroom (several sinks and one tub) and then, finally, bed.

Carole told me to kneel at my bedside to say my prayers.

'Prayers?'

'Yes. We have to say prayers every evening when we go to bed, and every morning when we get up. Kneeling at our bedside.'

How does one say prayers if one has never been taught or told to pray? I had, however, in the course of my five years at St Margaret's, learned the words of the Lord's Prayer. So that's what I prayed, kneeling obediently at my bedside: 'Our Father, which art in heaven…' (Why *which,* and not *who*, I occasionally wondered. I was a stickler for correct grammar.)

Now Miss Almond, all cheery and brisk, came bustling in with a 'Chop-chop, girls, all under the sheets!' Walking from bed to bed, she stuck a thermometer in all our mouths. A few minutes later she came around again, removed the thermometers, read each one, shook each one, stuck it back in the jar of disinfectant. This, I was to learn, was a ritual carried out every day, twice a day, for the first few days of school, either lined up in the front hall or in bed. I never questioned this ritual, but I presume it was to ensure that we started school all hale and healthy; after all, we came from all over the world, many of us from tropical countries with strange diseases such as malaria. After that was done, she wished us all goodnight, switched off the light, and left us to ourselves.

Lights out, and ordained silence. But how could I sleep, after all that had happened over the last forty-eight hours! The goodbye from Mum and Dad, Granny and Aunt Leila, the house and the yard, the animals and the babies. The suppression of tears, the determination to be brave, the long flight across the Atlantic. The Universal Aunt, the train ride to Harrogate, the white girl from Africa, the fairy-tale castle, Carole, Miss Almond, Killer, hordes and hordes of girls whose names I'd never learn! And now, silence, and the chance at last to digest it all. I had topsy-turvy feelings. Was I scared, or was I brave? Did I like it, or did I hate it? Would they like me, or would they hate me? Was Killer safe, or was she dangerous? What lay ahead?

It was all too much to contemplate, too much to digest. Just thinking about it all was exhausting. I fell asleep among the whispers and muffled giggles of the girls in the beds around me.

And so ended my first day at Oakdale School.

Chapter Twenty-Six

Food Anarchy

Dear Mum,

This is the letter I won't send you, the kind of letter I write in my mind. There are things I can't tell you out loud, because you would never understand.

People keep asking me if I miss you but I don't. They are trying to be kind. There is too much happening. I don't have time to miss you at all. I wonder if you miss me. I think you don't. I think you must be glad to have me out of the way because now you have more time to change the world. I think I was in your way the whole time.

But if I told you that it would hurt your feelings. I don't want to hurt your feelings so I won't tell you.

I will write you a real letter again next Sunday, when we have to write letters. But I won't tell you my problems. I won't tell you my one huge problem: the food here is terrible! Utterly disgusting! But you have to eat every single crumb. How will I even survive?

All my love, Jo

The days turned into a week. Chirpy Mummy Almond woke us all up early every morning, and the whole rigmarole started again. Temperature-taking, bedside prayer, washing, dressing. Bed-making.

I'd never made a bed in my life. Back in BG, bed-making consisted of untucking the mosquito net and knotting it into an overhead ball, which Mum or Aunt Leila did first thing, and then straightening the sheet, plumping the pillow, folding the top-sheet and laying it at the foot of the bed, which Aunt Leila did later in the morning. This was not my job. Here there was much more: a bottom-sheet, a top-sheet, a blanket, a pillow and an eiderdown, and it all had to be neat and tidy for inspection.

Hospital corners – what were they? Carole told me, and she may have taught me. They had to be perfect, neat triangles tucked under the mattress at each corner. The blanket had to be trimly turned down with the top-sheet and tucked into the mattress, with the eiderdown spread neatly on top of it all.

This was not the kind of task I'd ever be good at. It was just one of the ways in which I'd never take after my mother: practical matters demanding precision and an eye for tidiness. Sloppy hospital corners were to prove the bugbear of my life from that day onward. Thank goodness, these days, for duvets.

With our beds made and the inspections over, the day was ready to begin. We all trooped downstairs, single file, into the basement, where each girl had a locker with her games-and-outdoor wear, and it was time for Morning Run. One designated girl stood at the bottom of the stairs calling out what we were to wear that day for the Run, depending on the weather: 'Macs, caps and wellingtons!' Or, 'Macs, caps and game-shoes!' And later, on warm, sunny summer days, simply: 'Game-shoes!'

And off we'd sprint, three times around Miss Killingley's garden, a private enclosure set in the grounds. Every day, rain or shine, eighty-two girls would run or walk or limp or saunter around this garden and return to the locker-room, panting and groaning and griping: a healthy but much-detested start to the day.

More challenges followed, starting with breakfast. Before we picked up our cutlery, before we even took a sip of tea or put a morsel of food into our mouths, we said grace. That is, Killer, sitting at the mistresses' separate table on high, said grace: 'For what we are about to receive may the Lord make us truly grateful, for Christ's sake,' at which we'd all chant, 'Amen.' At the end of every meal, grace was said once again, but this time it went, 'For what we have received may the Lord make us truly grateful, for Christ's sake, Amen.' Dad would have been horrified.

For me though, new challenges followed mealtime grace. Every meal began in silence, and that was fine with me. But after a few minutes the mistress in charge would declare, 'You may talk now.' There I sat, that first day, physically and literally tongue-tied, looking left and right as all the girls broke into chatter around me. Carole was next-to-me-but-one, and I didn't know the girls sitting on either side of me. I huddled, while the talk swirled all around me, searching for something chirpy or brilliant or funny to say, but I was too slow, too worried about my speech to do so, and too polite to interrupt. And so the talk continued over my head.

Every day, we moved two places forward around the table, in either a clockwise or anticlockwise direction, and I was confronted with a new set of girls. And every day, Carole was my unavailable next-but-one.

Inevitably, the dreaded day came: my turn to sit next to the mistress at the head of the table, keeping watch over us all. That was the most terrible ordeal of all. And it was just as I expected. She turned to me, smiling, with those dreadful questions: 'How are you doing, Jo? Have you heard from your mummy and daddy yet? Are you homesick, Jo? Do you miss Mummy and Daddy? When will you be going home?'

But I was lucky. I mumbled something innocuous, but on her other side and opposite me was a chatterbox of a girl who managed to distract her enough to absolve me from conversation. I sat there in embarrassed silence, grateful for the reprieve. But worse was to come: butter.

Breakfast was a three-course meal. It started with cereal of some kind – cornflakes, Weetabix or Rice Krispies – with milk, followed by a cooked meal – eggs, bacon, baked beans – followed by bread, butter, and marmalade or jam. The worst of it all was the butter. I hated butter and had always hated it, especially smeared on bread. I didn't mind if things were *cooked* in butter, so you couldn't see it, but to spread it on bread – I thought it disgusting, vomit-inducing.

And so I sat there, playing with my knife and fork and a slice of soggy white bread. I left off the butter and nobody noticed that first day, but inevitably, one day I got caught. The beady eyes of a table mistress landed on me.

'Why aren't you eating butter, Jo?' she asked and there it was. I looked up at her with big, pleading eyes but I'd been caught in the act, with a slice of bread piled high with jam, sans butter.

The punishment, as ever, was fitted to the crime: I had to sit alone at a table in an empty dining room and eat two slices of bread thickly spread with butter. I almost gagged.

But there were even worse things to come, worse foods I had to force down my throat. Lunch was invariably grotesque. Day after day I faced the horror of struggling against the urge to vomit at full plates of substances disguised and offered to us as food. Day after day it was a slab of meat, which you could douse in gravy, some form of potato – boiled or mashed, or roasted on Sundays – and some form of probably tinned vegetable. Then there was the inevitable Monday fare, a dish masquerading as stew that we called 'chewed-up-and-spat-out', for obvious reasons – a name that implies I wasn't the only one who didn't appreciate it.

Other culinary highlights of the week came on Thursdays when we had liver, and Fridays when we had fish, boiled or battered. Worse than the fish, for me, was the invariable side dish of peas. Peas made me want to vomit. But you had to eat everything on your plate. You could ask for a 'small' portion, and, depending on the mistress serving at the head of the table, you might actually get a 'small'. And if by some strange distortion of your taste buds you wanted more, you could ask for seconds. But you *had* to have everything, and you *had* to finish your plate. No leftovers at all. And for me, eating even a 'small' was still a terrible ordeal.

Over time I developed my own methods of dealing with this unfortunate 'eat-everything' rule. In most cases, it was 'disguise and hold breath'. This worked for butter, spread thinly and buried under thick jam or marmalade so you could hardly taste it. It also worked for liver, the very smell and sight of which induced some serious gag reflexes. I dealt ingeniously with liver by cutting it up into tiny pieces and asking for extra servings of potato and veg, with which I smothered the tiny liver pieces, and washed it all down as quickly as possible with water. I was able to get away with this method all through my school life.

I wasn't so lucky with peas. I dealt with them creatively by clandestinely shoving them off my plate and into the napkin on my lap. I'd then covertly empty my napkin into my pocket and later on discard the peas in the toilet. But invariably, some of these hastily shovelled peas would land on the floor at my feet under the table, and one day my entire napkin slipped and emptied the full load on to the floor. There they all lay, scattered under and around my chair. Caught out! The punishment was to sit by myself at a table after lunch and eat a whole plate of peas. Peas, and nothing else. I don't know how I managed without vomiting.

The main course at lunchtime was always followed by a 'sweet'. That, in principle, was fine; I had a sweet tooth and there was nothing I loved more than desserts of all kinds. But Oakdale desserts, once again, failed the test. Very often we had to make do with a sickly-sweet pink blancmange. We also got chocolate stodge, steamed pudding served with slimy custard, semolina – and sometimes a chocolate version simply referred to as 'mud' – or sago, which we called 'frogspawn'. Another regular was 'earwax tart': pastry smothered with lemon curd; or jam roly-poly, aka 'dead-man's-leg'. Apple dumplings were 'boiled baby' or 'bottled baby', and Garibaldis – biscuits sprinkled with currants – were 'fly cemeteries'. We also got 'squashed flies', or mincemeat – the sweet kind – which reminded me of Tuesday lunch, which was usually minced beef slopped over slimy mashed potatoes. Not to be outdone, I invented my own terms: 'dried dog poo' for liver, and 'snotballs' for peas, all proving that ten-year-old girls are a pretty imaginative lot.

So much for lunch, which of course was invariably sandwiched between graces: giving thanks for what we were 'about to receive', and thanks, afterwards, for what 'we *had* received'. I joined in the chanted *Amen* at the end of pre- and post-meal grace, but I cannot tell a lie: I was not in the least grateful. A more honest grace in my case would have been, *Dear Lord, give me the strength and the resilience and the courage to face this meal,* and *Thank you for helping me survive the meal I've just partaken in.*

I did survive all those terrible meals. But forcing them down never cured me of that extraordinary pickiness when it came to food. I wished it was different, I wished I could down everything, including liver and peas, with relish. Indeed, I should have prayed for a love and gratitude for food, whatever it was, in a world where many children starved. A love and gratitude that was never granted to me.

There was one girl in that year, I think her name was Pamela, who was vegetarian, and was served special meals daily. I envied her with all my heart and wished that I, too, could be labelled vegetarian and thus be excused from the regular menu. But it never occurred to me to ask Mum – who would have certainly submitted such a request to Killer – or Dad.

Perhaps it was Dad's constant admonishments to 'finish your plate, think of the starving children all over the world!' that got me through the food ordeal, more so than the false appeal for gratitude. It was certainly more truthful. I did indeed know that I was lucky to have any food at all. The difference between home and here though was that at home I could choose what was on my plate and how much, and so eating it all up was a consequence of that choice. At school, there was never a choice. And yet I did it. I was not indulged. And the lesson I got from this is that you can't always get what you want. Exactly what Aunt Leila had taught me, but now put into practice.

Chapter Twenty-Seven

Banned Books and Lacrosse Sticks

Dear Mum,

Today is Sunday so I am writing to you again. I have to. Letter-writing time is after lunch. We all have to write letters home. They check. I am well. I hope you are well. I like my form teacher. Her name is Miss Hull. I am learning French from scratch, even though I already know a lot because you taught me French Without Tears. So I am very good at French, the best in class. My French teacher is Miss Brewer. I am going to write to Dad too. I don't know what else to say so I'll just say goodbye. Sorry this is so short.

Love, Jo

PS: There are no horses! No riding! That's terrible!

It was all so new, so strange. Here was I, a girl who had always run free, who had enjoyed the glorious liberty of a Montessori school, who had never been told what to do or what not, now thrown into a rigid system where every moment of the day was regulated and every task had to be performed *just so*. All movements here-or-there were preordained, and every diversion from the ordained path could earn you a private consultation with Killer. The very idea made me tremble with trepidation and induced me to good behaviour.

As I marched from place to place, following in Carole's footsteps like a little dog, upstairs and down, along the corridors single file, I noticed that some of the girls wore green badges bearing the word *Deportment*, and some wore red badges saying the same. Our daily uniform was a pleated tunic with a green girdle, worn over a white shirt and striped tie, but some girls wore blue girdles. Carole, as ever, explained it all.

'You get a green deportment badge for conduct. For not running or talking in the corridors and keeping a straight back, not slouching, not chatting in assembly and other quiet times, and tidy clothes. When you're really good, you get a red badge, and when you're really, really good, you get a blue girdle.' I determined to get all three. I was going to be on my best behaviour, and do my mother proud. It was what she would have done.

There are, indeed, advantages to being the kind of introspective, un-rowdy child I was. It took no effort to be virtuous. At the very worst, you might be branded a bore, which meant that the more boisterous girls disdained you, but that never actually bothered me. I'd never had rules before, and now they were all around me, and wonder of wonders: I enjoyed having rules. I enjoyed having a clearly defined structure; I needed that structure the way a vine needs a trellis to grow upwards. I liked having to monitor and amend my behaviour. And were it not for the food problem, I would have been in seventh heaven. In public Oakdale life, I was a goody-goody.

After breakfast, we all marched off to assembly. It started with us all lined up according to our forms in the central front hall, lines arranged by your height.

'We're going to be in Lower Third this term,' said Carole. The tiniest girls were in Lower Second, and were only eight years old. Lower Second was also the shortest line; I suppose few parents sent their daughters away to school at that tender age.

Then off we marched to the gym, where we sat in rows, again arranged by class, ready for the morning service. Killer strode on to the stage at the front, and the service began: a hymn, a Bible reading and a prayer, for which we knelt. One of the girls stepped up to the chancel to do the reading. I hoped and prayed that it would never, ever be me.

With assembly over, off we marched again, single file up and down the stairs, off to our classroom. The actual school day was about to begin, the reason for which we were all here. Education, with a capital E. I turned out to be the very youngest girl in Lower Third; my birthday in mid-September meant that I was not yet even ten. Carole and I were in Lower Third H – the H was for Hull, Miss Hull, my form teacher. And we were off.

After lunch came a quiet time, which started with *tuck*. Tuck was one of those words (along with *knickers*, *daffodils* and a few others) I'd never had reason to use back home, at least not in the present context. I knew about the careful tucking in of mosquito nets, or tucking your shirt into your waistband. Tuck, I now learned, was the local word for sweets. Luckily, books like the Malory Towers series had prepared me in advance for such alternative vocabulary.

Miraculously, I found that a tuckbox, filled to the brim with all kinds of sugary goodies, was at my disposal – another of the miracles Mum had arranged for from across the ocean.

'We can have three tuck a day,' said Carole, 'and six on Sunday. What'll you have? I'm having a Crunchie. It counts as three but it's the best.' I didn't know much about English tuck, but I soon learned, and I agreed with Carole: Crunchie *was* the best.

Duly replenished with tuck, I was delighted to find that now was a quiet time for reading. I could choose a book from the library shelves around the room and settle into one of the comfy-ish chairs. It was the first and only opportunity to read in the whole day, and with delight, I launched myself on the bookshelves. But another catastrophe lay in store: Enid Blyton books were absolutely banned!

You could not bring one of those horrors into school, on pain of confiscation – and perhaps burning? – and they were not supplied in the library. This was the first major disappointment, worse, even, than the food. Enid Blyton was my nourishment!

'Why?' I asked Carole. 'How can they ban books? What's wrong with them?'

She only shrugged. It was simply a fact of life. No Enid Blyton.

'I'm really looking forward to riding,' I told Carole. 'When do we have that?'

'Riding?' Her face was blank. 'I don't think anyone does riding here.'

'What! But that's the reason I came in the first place!'

She only shrugged. 'Maybe at senior school. We go there after two years.'

Instead of riding, we had games. After the afternoon session of lessons it was teatime. Off we trooped again, single file and in silence, down to the dining hall for a snack of bread, butter and jam. For me, it was another ordeal of disguising a gossamer-thin layer of butter under a thick coat of jam, and washing it all down with generous mouthfuls of tea. Then quick-march down into the basement, a quick change into games clothes – short-sleeved, open-necked Aertex shirts, short skirts, perhaps a sports jumper, and games shoes – and out on to the games field.

And so, a little brown girl from the tropics learned to play that quintessential girls' boarding school game: lacrosse. I learned how to cradle a lacrosse stick and run across the field in a gaggle of girls. I learned to pass the ball and shoot it into the net. I also learned netball, our other winter sport. As time would tell, I was not a sporty girl, not team material. Just one of those girls who would always be chosen last when teams were selected.

Chapter Twenty-Eight

The Gwens

Dear Mum,

I hope you are well. I am well.
    I like everyone here except the Gwens.

Love, Jo

Over the next few days and weeks Carole-with-an-e became my best
friend, perhaps my only friend. I'm not sure it was mutual, but she
at least tolerated my tagging on to her. But I liked the other girls
too, and though they probably found me a bit too reserved, and
thus boring, nobody rejected me. That was what I'd been afraid
of most: rejection. I'd been warned that white people didn't like
people like me. But I'd seen no signs of that, as yet.

Except for the two Gwens.

Both the Gwens were white girls from Africa, and they were
the best of friends, always together, a close-knit duo. Gwen S. was
from South Africa, Gwen R. from Rhodesia, today's Zimbabwe; or
perhaps it was the other way around. And I felt, I sensed, that they
were racist. I couldn't put my finger on the reason I believed this.
Maybe it was just a narrowing of their eyes when they looked at
me; or not looking at me at all. A slight wrinkling of the forehead,
maybe a disapproving sniff or two when they glanced my way. A

stiffening of the shoulders, imperceptibly pursed lips, a deprecating moue or two. A collection of almost invisible signs I might have been picking up on. Maybe I simply had an inner radar for an antagonistic attitude, which I interpreted as a reaction to my race. Or maybe I just had a chip on my shoulder. Certainly, in those early weeks there was no glaring act of meanness or rudeness on their part.

I'd already learned that being white or African did not automatically make you racist. I had countless white friends back in BG, starting with Sheila and Margaret, and that girl I'd met on my way to Harrogate that first day, Angela, had become a friend, and so had Jackie. In fact, Jackie was one of the warmest, friendliest, most admirable girls I met at Oakdale.

Jackie was from Nigeria, and of all my schoolmates she was the one I looked up to the most. She was short, blonde-haired and sturdily built, with an extraordinary gift for art and theatre, gifts that were fostered and developed at Oakdale. She was everything I'd like to be: outgoing, confident and, of course, talented, highly creative, as well as just plain *nice*. She was the kind of person people notice – not like shrinking-violet me. I considered myself lucky to have her as a friend. Jackie had a deep love of the country she considered home, and spoke with great sympathy of Black Africa. It was from her I first heard the word Biafra; although that tragedy was not to erupt until 1967, many years down the line, I remember her being concerned about it back then.

The two Gwens were of a different ilk to Jackie, and I sensed it. I normally had nothing to do with them and they were never in my small circle of friends but once, just once, Gwen S. showed her true colours. I had done something wrong, some stupid little thing, which angered or maybe just annoyed her. Her face turned bright red and she struggled to find an insult powerful enough to put me in my place.

'You're just – you're just…' she spluttered, and then she finally found the word she was looking for: 'you're just *brown!*'

When one thinks of a single dark-skinned girl in an all-white community, at a time when Britannia more or less still ruled the waves and America had not yet had its civil rights revolution, it's natural to think that that poor girl must have been ostracised, and must have felt like a fish out of water. She must have stuck out like a sore thumb.

But that wasn't the case. Perhaps it was because, not seeing myself from the outside and therefore unaware of this sore-thumb business, the fact that I looked different to everyone else never really bothered me. As a quintessential introvert, I was more concerned with consolidating my feelings of being uniquely myself, of figuring out exactly who I was and my constantly changing feelings as I reacted to the world around me, rather than analysing my physical place in the closed society in which I found myself. I didn't *feel* different. I didn't *think* of myself as different.

But Gwen's rebuke 'You're just *brown*!', spoken with such contempt, came as a shock, and it cut deep. It might seem harmless, and even amusing, but it startled me so much so that I never forgot it, and understood it instinctively as the insult it was meant to be. I never forgot the antagonistic, disdainful look in her eyes, the scorn in her face, the volumes of unspoken despisal hiding behind that innocuous word. The way she'd spat it out. She didn't have to say anything else. She didn't have to use profanities or four-letter-words or n-words. It was all contained in that one simple, innocent description.

Brown. I was brown, and nobody else was, and that one word, spoken with such haughtiness and scorn, put me as severely in my place as a barrage of insults hurled at me. *Brown.*

Different. You don't belong here!

After that, I knew to keep out of the way of the two Gwens. But there was more to it than looks. The Gwens, Jackie and Angela were not the only girls who came from overseas. There was also Margaret from Malaya, and tiny Rosemary from Singapore, and others from countries all over the British Empire. It was clear that they all came from prosperous families of the ruling class. And it was just as clear to me that I didn't. That I was from a lower category of humanity.

Nobody told me this. Nobody had to tell me. Nobody, neither a pupil nor a mistress, put me in my 'lower' place. There was no direct discrimination. It was something I felt in my bones: a sense of lowliness that was not inherent, but acquired through circumstances beyond my control. It was something subtle and elusive, yet very real to us all; a conventional wisdom imparted silently; an intuitive knowledge, if you will; a sense of one's place in the world. Something I knew I had to overcome.

It was a knowledge I instinctively felt was inherently, fundamentally wrong. Thanks mostly to my parents, I'd come this far believing that we are all created equal, irrespective of race, religion, sex or skin colour. I learned this, in defiance of the reality we lived in, a reality that demonstrated the very opposite: a clearly defined hierarchy, in which we are all slotted into a place that defines our destiny.

Resolving outer reality with inner realisation was the challenge facing me. Understanding that this reality existed, that things were as they were and that they weren't going to change for me, and that I had to learn to deal with them, just as they were: that was the challenge I lived with. How to live with that reality and overcome it internally became the trial of my life, and here in Harrogate I was practically in the lion's den. The stark reality of myself as an outsider forced me to understand that the only power I had was in my own reaction to that reality.

Back at home, we people of dark skin, we who lived on the lower rungs of society, below whites, at least we had each other. We were the majority, and we had companionship, family, warmth, joy and togetherness. We lived in our own company and could well ignore the reality of a stratified society with whites at the top, even if we knew we ranked lower. It really was only skin deep for us. We loved each other regardless of darkness or lightness of skin. We were all family.

Now, here, I was all alone. Gwen had put it all into one simple word that said everything. That word, *brown!*, spluttered in anger, went through me like a knife and told me everything. Everyone else was white, and we all knew, even if we never spoke it out loud, that I was different, and different in a negative way. I stood out. It is plain to see in all the school photos. I was that one girl who could immediately pick herself out from the crowd. The one dark face.

Harrogate Ladies' College, Lincoln House (East and West), 1964

But perhaps it was only my imagination? Was it only my own indoctrination that made me feel an outsider, different, and, yes, inferior? Was everyone else, apart from the Gwens, actually oblivious to me being different, and did I just have a chip on my shoulder, which that little word "brown" had brought into sharp relief?

I was too young to analyse it all, but I had to deal with it. I had to deal with the hurt, with that new sense of disorientation I had to find balance again, and I was alone, with nobody around I could talk it all through with.

I wasn't an introvert for nothing. I was used to working through my doubts and questions and the enigmas life posed on my own. For years now, I'd been trying to figure out what it was that made me essentially *me*. Was it my thoughts? My feelings? My personality? My dark body? What was a personality exactly, where did it come from, why did I have one, what *was* it? Where did that sense of 'me-ness' start, where did it end, and did everyone else feel 'me' exactly the way I did? Was the sense of 'me-ness' universal? Was it really just thoughts and feelings, all bundled up together? Who, exactly, am I?

These were the questions that had concerned and even plagued me ever since those early days when they'd first leaked into my mind, as I sat curled up before the air-conditioning unit in Federal House, Port-of-Spain. Questions that seeped through the conventional veneer of what I was supposed to believe, supposed to think. I was still trying to figure it all out, trying to define myself and my place in the world. Now, the question of being an inferior outsider became more pertinent than ever, but the answer was clear, and rose in me with the brilliance of sunlight.

No! I was not inferior! Even from an external perspective, I could see it for myself: here at school, the very point of which was scholastic achievement, the proof was glaringly obvious. I was every bit as clever and accomplished as my white classmates. I was already among the top pupils as far as marks were concerned. I constantly earned praise from Miss Hull for my essays, and from Miss Brewer for my French. My marks in those subjects were always top, and though I faltered slightly in arithmetic, I was nowhere near the bottom. Other, *white*, girls held that place. I could hold my own, scholastically, with all the white girls I was surrounded by, and especially so considering I was the youngest of them all.

But I lacked confidence, debilitatingly so. I'd soon realised that introverted children weren't appreciated, or even liked, as much as those outgoing, chatty, self-assured beings who could hold their own with adults as well as other children. Adults adored such children, and were at a complete loss with children like me, who they had to painstakingly prise open to draw a single word out of them. Children who behaved like closed clams and the more you pestered them, the more they closed down.

I wasn't that exuberant, gregarious child everyone liked. I wasn't among those who waved their hands wildly when a question was asked in class. Instead, I closed up. Nobody – no adult – was supposed to hear my voice. I couldn't speak in front of groups. A vast feeling of shame would overpower me, a fear that I'd be laughed at because my speech was slow and slurred and muffled. I couldn't rattle off information like they could. I admired no end all those whose personalities were carried on their spoken word, their clear voice; who could talk nineteen to the dozen, attract attention and hold it the moment they opened their mouths, mostly because they talked well. How I envied that ability! How I sank even more into myself when lost for words! And how my lack of confidence grew exponentially!

But as long as I could *see* words, words written on paper, or write them, I was fine. I could skim-read a poem or a text and grasp its gist immediately. I would learn it by rote in a wink and garner its meaning, even its hidden meaning. I could fit words together so that they made sense. I was good at spelling, meticulous when it came to grammar. Words were my stock-in-trade: as long as they were silent. Miss Hull was perceptive enough to let me learn in my own way, and gradually the other adults learned to leave me alone. They stopped trying to cure me of my shyness, or prise me out of my shell. They let me be, because the more they prised, the more I closed up.

They were well-meaning enough, those interrogations: *how are you, Jo? You're so quiet – are you all right? Do you miss your parents? Are you homesick? Are you unhappy?* Every now and then a teacher would smile kindly at me, pat me on the head, and ask me such invasive questions. I'd nod or shake my head appropriately, and wish they'd stop asking. I didn't want to be cross-examined. I didn't want to open up and disclose myself to those adults. I didn't want sympathy or, worse yet, pity. My thoughts and feelings were private. *Leave me alone!* I thought of any adult who trod too close.

I didn't want or need to be 'drawn out of my shell'. I wasn't *in* a shell, or if I was, that shell was porous, not closed off from the outer world. I was simply trying my best to work it all out by myself. My goal was ambitious enough: nothing less than to solve the mysteries of the universe on my own.

The term introspective is perhaps more apt than introverted, as it implies an actual internal investigation, a sorting-through of thoughts and feelings. Only with perspective and the wisdom of hindsight did this need to know myself ever become clear to me. Only since it synchronised perfectly with what was to become a lifelong quest have I been able to put that childhood reticence into perspective.

Now, at school, I was going it alone. And somehow I was quite happy in my little solitary world. I *knew* I wasn't defective. I just didn't know yet how to *behave* with such adults. How to ward them off but, at the same time, interact with them in a way that was neither rude nor disobedient. Luckily, there were many sensitive adults, like Miss Hull, who did leave me alone, did appreciate me for myself, and didn't try to pry. I adored her, in my own way, though I never showed it – I had no way of showing it.

Chapter Twenty-Nine

Hello Mater, Hello Pater

Dear Mum,

It's Sunday again so I'm writing you this letter. I have to, because we all have to write letters on Sunday, after lunch. Nothing much has happened. I am doing well. Today it is quite cold. We went for a walk to the Crag. I hope you are well. Say hello to Granny and Aunt Leila, and Aunt Elma and Mirri and Mervyn.

I'm sorry this letter is so boring. I don't know what else to write.

Love, Jo

Apart from the Gwens I now had several friends. Maybe it was because I listened attentively and adoringly to them. Or maybe it was because I had a distinct sense of humour, and loved to laugh. I giggled constantly, especially in that forbidden country of Lights Out, once Mummy Almond had plunged us into darkness. That's when we finally came alive, like mice coming out to play. I was an inveterate, unrepentant and irredeemable giggler.

Mostly, though, we just talked into the dark and giggled, always with one ear peeled for footsteps in the corridor outside or, worse yet, the doorknob turning. Whispers and giggles, stories from the comfort of your bed – what better way to sink into slumber?

Never let it be said that we Oakdale girls, marching silently along corridors, up and down stairs, all in our stiff green tunics and bearing red and green deportment badges or blue girdles, were turned into dreary stiff-upper-lipped clones by the discipline. Quite the opposite was the case. We were as creative and witty a bunch as ever did live. Sometimes a good trellis provides the best blooms. I needed the trellis, and I sang our very own Oakdale song as loudly as all the others. I even helped to make up new verses, sung to the tune of Allan Sherman's 'Hello Muddah, Hello Fadduh'. We loved to improvise, ever choosing new mistresses for new verses:

> *Hello Mater, hello Pater*
> *Here I am in Harrogater,*
> *And I'm writing*
> *You this letter*
> *In the hope that it will make me feel better.*

Then came the refrain, sung in a yearning wail:

> *Take me home! I promise to be good… Take me ho-o-o-ome…*
> *Don't like Matron*
> *Dirty hag's*
> *Confiscated*
> *All me fags*
> *She has put them*
> *On a shelf*
> *If I know Matron she will smoke them all herself.*
> *The sports mistress*
> *S'a good swimmer*
> *She says swimming*
> *Makes you slimmer…*

The rest of the song cannot be repeated for reasons of decorum and piety, but it's an example of the kind of creative output we set our minds to in those sacred dark minutes of Lights Out.

But even the mistresses were not all rules and regulations. They too had a sense of fun. There was one mistress, I think it was Miss Brewer, who took us for supper and always livened that meal up with a tale afterwards. She'd tell story after story, and they were invariably funny. Miss Brewer, or whoever it was, used to cycle to school every day, but one day her bicycle was stolen and was later found by a farmer in his field. So, we made up the following song for her:

> *Oh where, oh where did my little bike go*
> *Oh where oh where can it be?*
> *I heard it was found in a dirty ploughed field*
> *Oh deary, deary me!*

Chapter Thirty

The Bliss of Solitude

As the weeks passed I began to develop a deep aversion to arithmetic. Though I still managed to get adequate marks – 'adequate' being a six or seven out of ten – it didn't help that I didn't like the arithmetic teacher, Miss Surtees, who to my mind was a cold and boring fish. Or maybe arithmetic itself seemed cold and boring. I never could connect with numbers, and to this day I cannot retain them in my memory.

But Miss Surtees also took us for nature studies, and that was one of my favourite subjects, and mitigated somewhat my dislike of her. Nature studies was a hands-on subject. Off we'd go, into the glorious woods surrounding Oakdale, rain or shine, where Miss Surtees would explain all the miracles of flora and fauna. We learned about cuckoo's-spit, and frogspawn (which, of course, had always been my personal speciality). How to identify trees according to their leaves and bark, and the names of birds and flowers. I loved nature studies with a wholehearted and undivided love. It was a subject new to me, and I threw myself into it, body and soul. There we'd be, in our macs and wellies, tramping through the wetlands and woods surrounding the school, or down to the rushing beck at the bottom of the dale, gathered around Miss Surtees as she explained this or that. How could school ever get any better than that!

But it was Miss Hull who nurtured and guided my young mind in a direction that brought out the best. It was she who laid a foundation there that was to last me a lifetime. It was she who planted the seeds that were to grow into plants and continue to grow and flourish long after I'd left her behind. My favourite subject of all was English; the study of words, and what they could do. Words were magic. They created worlds within oneself, and you could lose yourself in those worlds.

Miss Hull was, and would be for evermore, a teacher after my own heart. I adored her, and adored her lessons. Together, she and the class explored books, discussed books, wrote about books, drew pictures about books – what could be more satisfying than that! I still possess, in a crumbling and dilapidated form, one of the projects we did, either in that year or the following.

'Girls,' said Miss Hull one day, 'we're going to do something exciting. You're going to make a little book yourself. That's going to be our term project, and you can design it all on your own. I want to see your best handwriting. I want you to choose your favourite passages, and draw pictures from the book. Marks out of ten!'

The project was to be based on the book *Tarka the Otter*, by Henry Williamson. Our brief was to design and create our own little booklet on Tarka. We were to choose extracts and favourite quotes from the story and write them on white paper in our best handwriting, then paste them into the green, A4 light-cardboard 'book'.

I plunged into the work. I read through the book again, chose my favourite passages, drew pictures, cut and pasted them into the pages next to the passages. I chose descriptive passages, not action sequences; not one of the scenes in which Tarka is hunted by predators, animal and human; in which the huntsman's horn strikes fear into his heart. I chose passages where language seduces us to feel and live Tarka's wonderful environment, my main inspiration; nature described in evocative words. I simply loved words and was intrigued by how they could evoke entire worlds.

My Tarka the Otter booklet is the only thing remaining from my Oakdale days; crumbling at the edges, falling apart at the seams, it is though still intact, along with Miss Hull's marks on the back: a big fat *Good* beside her marks, all in the meticulously neat script she was known for. The marks were given for Cover, Writing, Drawing and Imagination; my best mark was 10/10 for Imagination, but I only got 7+/10 for Writing. Miss Hull's standards must have been extraordinarily high as my handwriting, to me today, seems just about perfect for a ten-year-old.

One of my favourite exercises in English was when Miss Hull gave us a list of ten random words out of the dictionary, and asked us to write an essay using all of them – but it had to make sense. It couldn't be a nonsense essay. I loved that, and was good at it: I got top marks as a matter of routine. But to stand up in class and answer a question relating to something we'd just learned? No. I'd go all hot and bothered and the words would stutter out and not make sense. As long as the work was in writing, though, I was perfectly fine.

Miss Hull made us learn poems off by heart, poems from that classic school-book, *The Dragon Book of Verse*. One by one we learned them: 'I Wandered Lonely as a Cloud', and 'The Rime of the Ancient Mariner', and 'The Tyger'. And my very best favourite, 'Sea Fever' by John Masefield:

I must go down to the seas again, to the lonely sea and the sky,
  And all I ask is a tall ship and a star to steer her by;
And the wheel's kick and the wind's song and the white sail's shaking,
  And a grey mist on the sea's face, and a grey dawn breaking.

A poem that not only addressed my own deep love of the sea, it also evoked memories of that unforgettable day at Blanchisseuse. The beautiful rhythm, the pacing, the use of words sank deep into my subconscious and taught me an innate sense of the power of words and how they fit together to create beauty. Learning poetry, especially classical poetry, by heart is a method that seems to be falling out of favour, yet there is no better way to nurture good writing, especially if it is done at a young age. We absorb through these poems a deep sense of how words can work like musical notes, creating melodies that resonate with others. Words skilfully arranged draw pictures, create scenes, evoke feelings, move hearts and minds. If it is true that the pen is mightier than the sword, then there's no better way of wielding that pen than by absorbing the timeless words of those who have mastered their use. This is the way future writers are made.

In these poems I often found echoes of my own peculiarities. Take the last verse of 'I Wandered Lonely as a Cloud':

> *For oft, when on my couch I lie*
> *In vacant or in pensive mood,*
> *They flash upon that inward eye*
> *Which is the bliss of solitude;*
> *And then my heart with pleasure fills,*
> *And dances with the daffodils.*

William Wordsworth *got it*. He *understood*. The bliss of solitude! Yes! Wasn't that what I was seeking? Wasn't that the distant calling? Wasn't that exactly what Blanchisseuse was all about?

Chapter Thirty-One

Drinking the Opium

Sundays were different. It started with getting dressed, not in the everyday tunic and tie, but in the dark green serge dress with clover collar in which I'd arrived at school that first day. Breakfast was different, too: boiled eggs in eggcups. And after breakfast, no lessons, but marching off to chapel at senior school. We walked in crocodiles, two by two, with a mistress at the rear, accompanied by two pupils. It seemed like an endless walk, back then, though I now know that it's less than five minutes from Kent Road to Clarence Drive.

Oakdale girls had their own reserved pews along the nave, all facing the aisle. At my first visit I stared in awe as the big girls from college all trooped in, filling their own pews, shorter girls to the fore, taller ones at the back. The mistresses had their own section up in the balcony. Apart from the shuffling of shoes as everyone edged sideways into place, a reverent hush lay over us all. To the right, the beautiful stained-glass windows in the chancel provided the only light, lending to the atmosphere of hushed sanctity. I never failed to feel the effect myself: a sort of sinking into myself, a calming of thoughts, a sense of deep peace . I had never known that sense before, having never been taken to church.

Last of all, the choir trooped in: two rows of senior girls all clothed in green and red robes, walking slowly up the aisle to the chancel, slipping into their own spaces beneath the tall panels of stained glass. Then the service began, led by Miss Todd, the senior school headmistress, who I was seeing for the first time. Miss Todd was a grey-haired lady of stature in all senses of the word: tall, slim and dignified and with an arresting voice and a well-defined face.

Sunday service involved three hymns, a Bible reading, a sermon by Miss Todd and a canticle by the choir. This might be the Magnificat, or the Agnus Dei, or the Te Deum and Benedictus. Whichever it was that first day, it completely swept me away. Those voices, raised in such sweet and perfect harmony! Like it or not, my heart was touched and there was nothing I could do to deny it.

I never told either of my parents that Harrogate Ladies' College, and its appendage Oakdale School, were deeply embedded in Church of England doctrine. I never told them that daily prayer, grace at the table, obligatory bedside prayers, New Testament readings and hymns were our daily fare, and triple that on Sundays. I knew exactly what they'd both say to that. I could hear my father's cry of protest: this was exactly the kind of indoctrination he'd prohibited for me! It went against everything he'd ever taught me. He'd call it brainwashing. *Religion is the opium of the people!* Mum would call it coercion. They'd be appalled. Perhaps they'd remove me from the school. And that was why I never told them. Enjoying chapel was a little protest of my own. It was part of my internal need to find my own way through the labyrinth of ideology versus truth. To find my own internal being. I had wobbled all my life. This was a new adventure.

Left to myself, I had only my own instinctive reactions to go by, and those were all not only positive but overwhelmingly so. Was it brainwashing, this deep sense of peace and reverence that washed through me, not only at the sound of that singing but induced by the very atmosphere of that chapel? I couldn't help it. It was just *there*, and I felt it, and it was deep and enduring.

The same thing happened, to a lesser degree, during our daily assemblies at Oakdale. I went willingly through all the rituals and

I prayed the prayers. I sincerely prayed the Our Father, kneeling every morning and evening at my bedside, and even adding little personalised prayers of my own.

We learned other prayers off by heart. The Oakdale school prayer, for instance.

> *Almighty God, the Father of us all, look with Thy loving favour upon our school and grant to all its members to be truthful, pure, obedient, kind and gentle, that following the example of Thy holy child Jesus we may come at last to our home in heaven, through Jesus Christ our Lord, Amen.*

And, more formally, the Apostles' Creed, chanted at every Sunday service, for which we all had to stand and turn to face the altar, a moment of deep reverence: *'I believe in God the Father Almighty, maker of heaven and earth…'*

But it was the hymns, especially, that brought forth a soaring sense of joy and well-being. Hymns that urged us to *Lift up your hearts! We lift them Lord to thee!* How could I not grow wings and soar along with the chorus of children's voices?

I was hooked. *Captured*, Dad would say. Brainwashed perhaps? I certainly had a sense of deep serenity, a sense of being *grounded* in something other than my fledgling personality. Something profound, mysterious, and deeply fulfilling. Something beyond reason. In feeling this way I was rebelling against my own father.

Dad was hard-wired as an atheist, and from an early age he had coached me in all the atheist arguments in existence. 'There's no God!' he insisted, 'it's all a fairy tale! Religion is control of the people!' For me, this was food for thought. And even back then, aged six and seven, I did think about it. A lot.

Since Dad encouraged all his children to think for ourselves and question everything, I did just that: I questioned his views on God and religion. I had no particular religious teaching to tell me otherwise. All I had was Aunt Leila's demonstrated devotion, the story of Jesus's birth at Christmastime, the bits and bobs of Christianity I picked up here and there, and the brightly coloured, stylised and slightly kitschy pictures of Hindu gods I'd see on the stalls when Aunty took me to Stabroek Market. I had an open mind, and if there was any bias at all, it came from him: the absolutism of his conviction and his arguments. Is there a God, or isn't there? If so, who, or what, was He/She/It?

God was an enigma I was determined to solve, but I was not about to ask adults for a solution. I knew Dad's argument, and Aunt Leila's faith, and Mum's indifference to the whole matter, so I knew I had to figure it out by myself. Dad had always emphatically urged me to think for myself: question everything, doubt everything they told me about God and Jesus and life after death. And so, obediently, I began to question him as well.

The very word God, back in BG, had filled me with an indescribable sense of awe. I knew what the word meant, or what it was supposed to mean, and what it encompassed: the creator of *everything*. This world, all the people and animals and insects, the whole universe, the stars and planets, since the beginning of time. Something so majestic, so magnificent, so all-knowing, so powerful, we as paltry humans would be incapable of ever figuring it out.

So when Dad told me the existence of God couldn't be proven, I only thought, well, *of course* not! To try to prove the existence of *that* would be like an ant trying to prove the existence of humans! And when Dad argued that science disproved the existence of God, I'd reflect: if God is who they say He is, then surely He would have invented and created science too, and its laws? How could an invention, science, ever prove the existence of its inventor and creator? Obviously, I did not express those thoughts in those words, but this was my childish reasoning.

And when Dad argued that there were many religions, so obviously they couldn't all be right, my little mind thought, *why not*? What if they all worship and honour the same power, but in different ways? After all, people are different, *we* are different, all over the world. Why couldn't that power, if it exists at all, allow different approaches, like different paths up the same mountain?

And I wondered: is God a person, just like us? An imaginary man up in the sky, like Dad said? It couldn't be, I thought. A man in the sky would be too small for all that is attributed to him – all the power, all the wisdom, all the love. It *has* to be more. An enigma too big for a mere human mind to grasp, far too grand for us to reason out.

That, in the end, was my conclusion. It was all far too enormous for us to possibly comprehend. Too much to know for little me, only ten years old. But I questioned, I probed, and I *wanted* to know. To really *know*, beyond a doubt. But there were no final answers. My brain – my mind – was too small. Mum was right: admit you don't know, and stay away from it all. I became an agnostic at nine years of age, even before I set foot in England. But my mind was open, and ready to latch on to any explanation I could find.

Now, I couldn't believe that God was a man up in the sky who judged us and sent us to hell or heaven. But I felt *something*. A power, and a sense of overwhelming awe. It wasn't something that could be proven or argued for, but it was definitely *there*, and it had gripped me, unprepared as I was, so that I could sink into it and simply feel it. Little by little, I felt my inhibitions and the tight ball of insecurity within me melting in a deep feeling of *being*, grounded in something bigger than that little knot I called *me*. It was an undeniable calling. *Come, and drink, and you shall be sated.* That was the call, and it was irresistible. I had to follow.

And so, in the weeks that followed, I joined the voluntary session of Sunday School that took place after lunch back at Oakdale. We were divided into three subgroups called, for some strange reason, the Merry Mini-Minors, the Rollicking Rolls-Royces and the Bouncing Bentleys. I was a Merry Mini-Minor, and with all the other happy cars I joined in the singing of songs such as 'The Wise Man Built His House upon a Rock', 'He's got the Whole World in His Hands' and 'All Things Bright and Beautiful', led by a very enthusiastic scripture mistress. She also told us stories from the New Testament and gave us inspiring little lectures. Although these sessions were held during my precious free time, subtracting from my rare reading time, I never missed one of them. I especially enjoyed learning the 'Sixty-Six Books Song', in which we named and sang all the books of God's Holy Word, starting with Genesis and ending with Revelation. I've since discovered, to my amazement, I can still sing that song – apart from a stumble over *Ephesians, Galatians, Philippians* – from beginning to end.

Dad would have been incandescent. He would have snatched me away. It felt almost like a rebellion, a little private revolt of my own.

But our – perfectly voluntary – Sunday School attendance would one day be rewarded. The following summer, quite without pre-warning, the entire class was treated to a barbecue at an orphanage or some similar charity – an unforgettable day out. Was it bribery? I don't believe so, because it was all a surprise. None of us knew in advance of the treat awaiting us. It was a reward for our voluntary faith, and it was the best day of the school year.

Chapter Thirty-Two

Joint Letters

Dear Mum,

*This is a joint letter. Carole and I are going to write exactly
the same thing to our parents every week. Here goes:*
    *I hope you are well. I am well. This week we had to learn
'The Rime of the Ancient Mariner' by heart. Elizabeth C.
had to read it out at assembly. This morning it was raining
so we wore macs, caps and wellingtons for Morning Run.
That is all. Nothing else happened.*

Love Jo

'I have an idea,' said Carole, one Sunday, as lost for inspiration
as I was. We were writing our usual Sunday letters home, but the
letters were getting shorter and more boring week by week. 'Let's
both write exactly the same letters, every week!'

I jumped at the idea. 'What shall we write?' I asked as we both
sat down at the table, pen in hand. It turned out, brilliant as the
idea had seemed, that when it came to content there wasn't much
more you could put in a joint letter than in a single one. For a
week or two, we both wrote the very same, very short and boring
letters home. It was one way to combat the monotony of Sundays.
We soon dropped the idea; in my case, there were goings-on at

home I had to respond to, and in her case, there was an exeat to look forward to.

I was beginning to notice more and more the difference between me and the other girls. It wasn't just that we looked different, it was also that most of them had parents or relatives in England, while mine were far away, across the ocean. This was particularly noticeable at exeat and half-term time.

In the weeks between the start of term and half-term came an exeat weekend. Girls' parents and guardians swooped in and out and took them out for the day, on either the Saturday or the Sunday. The distance to my own guardian – Mrs Williamson of Cumberland, whom I'd not yet met – was too far for her to drive, for an exeat or even for half-term. So I'd be stuck at school.

Luckily, Carole's parents came to the rescue. They invited me to come out on Carole's first exeat, and I spent a delightful day with a proper family. I'm ashamed to say that I was probably not a very good guest, reverting to my usual closed-as-a-clamshell silence with the adults. But they were kind people and did their best, and the fact that they continued to invite me out for one exeat a term over the two years I spent at Oakdale indicates, perhaps, that they did not write me off as an incredibly rude child. I would never be chatty with adults, but I had been taught politeness even in silence, and that, perhaps, was my saving grace.

Carole's family took us to lunch at the Old Swan Hotel, Harrogate's most well-known restaurant. I had scampi for lunch, which I will never forget because I'd never had scampi before and it was utterly delicious – the best full meal I'd ever had in my whole life.

Later in the afternoon we had high tea at Bettys, another unforgettable occasion. Carole and I returned to school that evening, our stomachs replete with delicious food, and braced for more weeks of chewed-up-and-spat-out and, for me, weekly dried dog poo and snotballs. But scampi went down in my personal annals as my favourite all-time dish, the gold standard of all regular meals. Especially if served at the Old Swan Hotel in Harrogate.

At half-term everyone had to go home, and I was still homeless. But with her signature efficiency Mum had, once again, made appropriate arrangements. Once more, I was allowed to choose the paid foster-family with whom I'd spend the holiday. I chose a vicar's family in Nottingham, because I loved Robin Hood and maybe I thought I'd run into him. To me, it seemed a reasonable choice and I had a good but forgettable time.

Chapter Thirty-Three

Home Thoughts from Abroad

As much as I hated writing letters home, I loved receiving them. Mum and Dad both wrote to me every week, filling me up with goings-on back at home: family affairs, births and birthdays. But one day, Mum wrote me something very disturbing that made me anxious.

In August of 1961, the month before I'd left for England, general elections had been held in BG and had resulted, again, in a victory for the People's Progressive Party headed by Dad's hero, Cheddi Jagan. Before that, the party had split, with Jagan's one-time comrade-in-arms, Forbes Burnham, forming his own party, the People's National Congress (PNC). A third party had also been formed: the United Force (UF), a conservative party representing big business, the Roman Catholic Church and Amerindian, Chinese, English and Portuguese voters.

The majority of PPP voters were Indian. The majority of PNC voters were Black. The colony was now split clearly down the middle along racial lines. Through effusive and concerned letters Dad, a consummate PPP supporter in spite of being the 'wrong' race, kept me informed of everything that went on. I might have been only ten, but he explained this all to me in ten-year-old terms.

'The PPP won the election! By a landslide! A landslide is when there's a huge gap between the front runner and the next, like when you run a race with someone much slower than you.'

The PPP had gained twenty seats, compared with eleven seats for the PNC and four for the UF, he explained.

Both Mum and Dad informed me of the resulting unsettled political situation through their letters, each with a different slant. Mum wrote:

> *Darling, things are getting very hot over here since you left, and a bit dangerous. You know the United States has an embargo on communist Cuba, don't you? That means they can't trade with Cuba. But now Che Guevara – that's one of Cuba's leaders – has offered BG loans and equipment, and Jagan has accepted. Jagan also signed trade agreements with Hungary and the German Democratic Republic (East Germany). Your father is becoming more and more embroiled in far-left politics. It's not safe here any more. I'm so glad you're out of the country.*

Dad, on the other hand, wrote:

> *The British and American governments are getting really worried! They think British Guiana is on the brink of becoming another Marxist hotspot in the Americas, another Cuba! They can't allow that, of course. We're worried they're going to send in the army. That would mean civil war!*

Civil war for BG, Dad explained, meant a war between the two majority races, Indians and Africans. And it was racial tension, more than leftist ideology, that mobilised the main opposition party, Burnham's PNC. He drifted into adult language, which I could hardly follow, but he was angry and he wanted me to know. 'It's a destabilisation campaign conducted by the PNC!' he wrote. 'Riots and demonstrations against the democratically elected PPP! And it is all encouraged and supported by the imperialist forces of the British and American governments! They are supporting that corrupt scoundrel, Burnham!'

Just as he had given me a firm anti-religion grounding, Dad thought I should receive an early grounding in politics. This was the way for me to develop a social conscience. All this was conveyed through his long, barely legible, handwritten letters.

The Black PNC, he said, opposed the PPP on racial grounds, while the UF opposed it on ideological grounds. Britain, meanwhile, was enjoying the chaos. It was divide and conquer. 'The British Government wants to unseat Jagan!' Dad complained. A week of strikes and riots would shake the city of Georgetown in mid-February 1962, all of which I was kept informed of through Dad's letters.

Meanwhile, Mum was only concerned and grateful that I was far away, in England: 'Thank goodness you're not here!' she wrote. 'People are being attacked in the street for their political affiliation. It's complete chaos! Your father is a PPP man – they might have targeted you!'

After a few weeks of anarchy the British authorities put down a heavy and final boot. They sent in the troops; British soldiers swarmed through Georgetown. The governor declared a state of emergency. And to cap it all, the country's electoral system was changed to use proportional representation, under which Jagan could no longer win.

In a way I was glad I wasn't there to witness it all – who wants to live in a country at war with itself? On the other hand, I wished I was at home: I was missing all the excitement, history in the making! Here I was, stuck in a fairy-tale castle where I was more a prisoner than a princess. Some people might say this was a nice problem to have, whisked away to safety before matters at home got really bad. Yet I was only marginally interested in the explosive situation at home – what ten-year-old can really imagine a country at war with itself? I was only worried for my family. Were they safe?

'Don't do anything dangerous, Daddy!' I wrote. 'Please don't fight with the British Army!' I imagined him walking out to face the army all on his own, like in the cowboy films we'd watched. It was one thing being far away and safe myself, but what would happen to them?

'Mummy, please don't walk the streets, or ride a bike! Take a taxi to work!' I wrote to my mother.

They both reassured me that they were safe, and would stay safe.

In the meantime, Dad and Faye had had a new baby, another boy, named Gary. The family was growing, and his main concern was them. He would not get involved in anything risky, he assured me. I was not to worry.

Mum had been reassuring me from the start of the unrest. 'Please don't worry, darling. It will all be over soon,' she wrote before the end of the Christmas term. 'Please concentrate on your studies. Christmas is drawing near and you'll be off to Cumberland. I do hope you like Mrs Williamson. At last you'll be able to ride. I bet you can't wait for the holidays! But I shall miss you dreadfully!'

Indeed: I could hardly contain my patience as the second half of that first term took its leisurely time. I was by now a seasoned pupil who knew the ropes. It was all routine now: assembly, lessons, terrible food, lacrosse, tuck, letters home, bedside prayers. As Christmas and the winter holidays drew near, excitement began to mount within me.

I'd be going to Mrs Williamson's place in Cumberland for Christmas.

That meant, at long last: horses. And riding.

Part Four

England 1963–64

My Friend Flip

Chapter Thirty-Four

Summer Hill

'Hello Jo! Lovely to meet you!'

Mrs Williamson met me in the hallowed lobby outside Killer's office, now crowded with girls meeting their parents, cries of welcoming glee coming from both sides. But I was a special case, as I was to be whisked away, once again, by a perfect stranger. And as usual, that niggling sense of being a misfit overcame me. All the other girls seemed to have someone who really cared, and I was going off to a paid carer. But it was what I'd wanted, wasn't it? I'd wanted ponies. And at last, I'd be with them and I'd learn to ride. A dream was about to come true.

Killer summoned me and duly handed me over, having established the stranger's identity. Somehow, Mum had gone through all the required paperwork, and this woman now bending down and holding out her hand for me to shake was to be my legal guardian for the entire rest of my school life. I silently took the proffered hand and shook it.

She looked puzzled. 'Where's your suitcase?' she asked.

'Oh, Jo doesn't have any home clothes!' explained Killer. 'She arrived in her uniform and we didn't think it would be necessary to pack any school clothes.'

'Well, we'll have to deal with that at home. Come along then, Jo!' Mrs W. took my hand and led me through the milling crowd out into the drive and across to the car park, dodging all the vehicles slowly edging away or arriving to park, the parents and girls chattering to each other excitedly as they made their way to freedom.

We arrived at her car, a green Morris Minor station-wagon with wooden fittings. 'This is Frances!' said Mrs Williamson, introducing me to the car. 'She's an old friend, and pleased to meet you!'

She kept up the banter all the way home. Mrs Williamson was a short, stocky, wiry, brisk sort of woman, the kind of person who is never short of small talk, who doesn't notice when her conversational partner does not engage in the conventional back-and-forth of light banter. As ever, I was too shy to say a word, interjecting only enough requisite yesses and noes to keep the dialogue at a basic polite level.

On the way home she told me about her establishment. In winter, she told me, she'd have no guests. I'd be the only child. 'The others will be coming in the Easter and summer holidays,' she explained, 'and it'll be more fun for you then.' That was disappointing; would I be cooped up with an adult for the next few weeks?

'But there are lots of ponies!' she said, 'and you'll get to know them all, and take care of them!' That cheered me up immediately, until she said, 'But no riding, I'm afraid. The riding starts at Easter, when the guests come and we start with lessons. You won't be able to ride until you've had lessons.'

'Oh!' was all I said to that. More waiting yet! But what could I do but nod understandingly and accept another long wait until my dream came true – the very purpose of my coming to England?

On the way to Cumberland we passed through towns called Giggleswick and Wigglesworth. 'Shall we have a wiggle at Giggleswick or a giggle at Wigglesworth?' she jested, and went on to make every possible word variation between the words giggle, wiggle, worth and wick. It was to become a running joke on all our future trips between Summer Hill and Harrogate. I found it funny, and laughed along, but crippled by shyness, I never offered my own suggestions.

After what seemed to me an interminable road trip, we arrived at the village of Silecroft, on the Cumberland coast. She turned the car off the main road onto what seemed little more than a country track cutting through fields undulating into the distance, fields bare of trees but dotted with cows and sheep. To our left, beyond the fields, stretched the Irish Sea, grey water merging into the grey of the sky.

'On a clear day you can see the Isle of Man!' she told me. 'And beyond that, Ireland!' She chuckled. 'No, I'm only joking. You can't *ever* see Ireland.'

For now, though, she warned me, 'There'll be a few gates to open,' and very soon we arrived at the first. I lugged open the heavy six-barred gate and she drove through. I closed the gate after her and got back into the car. On we drove. This happened several times as we crossed fields in which cattle and sheep grazed, open farmland and bleak winter-green hills rolling off towards the horizon.

Finally, we drove through the gates of Summer Hill and came to a stop. 'Welcome to your new home!' she said.

The house was a sprawling, low-pitched white building that seemed not to have a front door. Mrs Williamson led me through a shed-like building on whose walls were mounted multiple saddles of all sizes, bridles hanging from pegs, halters and metal paraphernalia such as stirrups and metal bits dangling from hooks. There was a large sink, buckets piled in a corner, closed bins, and multiple show ribbons – red, yellow, green and blue – pinned to any free space on the walls. The smell was a melange of leather, grain and something a bit greasy and soapy.

'This is the tack-room,' she told me as we passed through to the shed's back door. From there, a short path led to the back of the actual house. As Mrs Williamson opened the door, a wriggling black dog leapt up to welcome first her, then me.

'This is Cubby,' said my guardian, 'and I can see you're going to be great friends.'

I fondled Cubby as I followed her into what seemed to be a rather dark and cluttered utility room. A further door led to a very warm and cosy, but quite small, kitchen, with a table and four chairs. Tucked into a corner of the kitchen was a large cream-coloured stove – the Aga, emitting a cosy warmth.

Going through the kitchen we came to the house proper, with stairs leading up to the first floor, onto a landing interrupted by several closed doors with names on them. She opened a door labelled Skye. 'This will be your own room at Summer Hill,' she told me. 'Make yourself at home, settle in, and come down when you're ready. I've made some soup and I'll warm it up on the Aga.'

It was a small bedroom, with a view over the yard we'd just walked through and the tack-room. Beyond the enclosing walls, the bleak landscape stretched away to the horizon: softly rolling hills, dreary and bare, sectioned off by wooden fences, and in the distance a low building that looked like another shed. The view was all rather desolate. The room was cold.

A deep sense of alienation, loneliness even, overcame me. Coming to this remote place was a huge leap from the hustle and bustle of school. It was scary. There were no children anywhere in sight, only this one friendly but very talkative woman, who never let up for a moment to actually tune in to me to learn what sort of a person I was, to get to know me. She commanded the relationship; it was up to me to tune in to *her*, not the other way around.

But I was a child used to solitude, who loved silence. There would be more than enough of that here. And looking around the first room of my very own I'd ever had in my entire life, I noticed at once that I wouldn't be lonely for a day. I was surrounded by friends of a different kind: books! Bookshelves, on all the walls, completely filled with books! The room, the entire place, may have been bleak and cold, and I may not have had anyone to talk to, but books would supply all my needs – if they were the right kind of books.

A closer look told me that they were all children's books, and my heart swelled. I knew that I'd be right at home here. Books, and ponies. What more could I ask for? I might not have physical friends here, but I'd never be without company.

Later, Mrs W. came to my room and asked me to follow her. She took me to what appeared to be a kind of storeroom, and opened a chest. It was full of used children's clothes. We had to kit me out, she explained. 'These are clothes my riding-school children grew out of and left behind,' she said. 'We'll definitely find something to fit you.' Sure enough, I was soon the proud owner of a whole new set of old trousers, jumpers, shirts, anoraks and jodhpurs.

'That's a good start!' Mrs W. said approvingly as I tried them all, one after the other, and made my choice. 'We don't want you wearing new clothes for outdoor work with the ponies. But you'll need some nice new things too. We'll do that tomorrow. Maybe a nice dress, for the Christmas party.'

A nice *dress*? Over my dead body, I thought, but as always, I kept those subversive thoughts to myself. I didn't want to upset her on my first day. And there was a party to look forward to. Perhaps there I'd meet some children.

Chapter Thirty-Five

Pony Heaven

Dear Mum,

It's my first night at Summer Hill. Mrs W. is strange. She talks all the time, telling me things. I never know what to say so I don't say anything. I have not seen a single pony yet. And she told me there isn't any riding in the winter but I can help take care of the ponies. I look forward to that.

Everything is strange. But don't worry about me. I am fine. (Do you ever worry about me?) I hope you are well and doing lots of good work.

I keep thinking of the warm sun in BG. And Christmas around the corner. And you. I suppose you are working hard. Sometimes I do get homesick. Mrs W.'s daughter is coming next weekend. I didn't ask what age she is. I hope she is about my age.

Love, Jo

The following day I got to meet the ponies. Awakened by Mrs W. and rubbing the sleep out of my eyes, I pulled on some clothes and made my way downstairs. Mrs W. led me out the back and into the fields. It was early. So early, in fact, that it was still dark, and she held a torch. 'This is how we start the day at Summer Hill,' she explained. 'The ponies have to be brought in and fed.'

I was beyond excited, in spite of the early hour and the darkness. This was to be my very first encounter with the real, living ponies who were, I was sure, to become my friends in a way that those magnificent steeds at the Mounted Branch never could. My heart pounding with the thrill of it all, I followed her as we trampled across the paddock closest to the house, out of a gate next to the building I'd seen the day before, which turned out to be an open stable. A wild, rough wind was blowing in from the sea, so strong I had to battle to even stay upright. It howled around the building and whipped at my clothing. I dug my hands into my pockets and swore to wear gloves outside in future. We crossed another paddock and came to a large, six-barred gate. Behind the gate stood the ponies, of all shapes and sizes and colours. The only thing they had in common was that they were all, every one of them, shaggy, their winter coats protecting them from wind and weather.

They grunted and shuffled as we approached, obviously excited. Together, Mrs W. and I shoved open the gate, an easy matter as the blistering wind helped push it open. The ponies shuffled backwards, obviously used to this routine. Some of them shoved their noses at Mrs W., who laughingly dug her hands into the pockets of her anorak and pulled out palms full of horse-nuts, which she fed to this snuffling nose or that. 'Hello, my darling!' she said to each one. 'Good morning, Sunny! Good morning, Lucky! Hello, Flip!'

Once the gate was fully opened the ponies plodded through, after which we closed it again, together. This time, the wind was against us. The gate pushed back, and it took all my strength to press it back into closed position. 'Always close gates after yourself, when you live in the country!' Mrs W. warned. 'It's the law of the land.'

Once all the ponies had been herded into the stable we set about stuffing hay into hay-nets, hanging them well spaced out along

the walls so that each pony had its own net. Soon, the sound of
satisfied chomping filled the air. The ponies were happy, and so
was I. In fact, I was thrilled. This was it! I breathed in the smell of
them, shoved my nose into their manes, rubbed their noses and
nuzzled them. I loved every minute I spent with them. This was
the heaven I'd dreamed of for so long. Now, if only I could ride
them as well – gallop across the fields, their manes and tails flying
out in the wind – my ecstasy would be complete.

That, of course, was an impossible dream. I was a long way
away from flying on horseback across the landscape. And that
angry, blistering wind didn't really encourage the notion of manes
and tails flying – it was more like me being blown away across the
countryside. I could hardly even stand upright in it. The dream
was a long way away from coming true.

The rest of that morning, apart from a quick breakfast break, I
was sucked into the heaven that all pony lovers know. I learned the
names of those wonderful creatures: Lucky and Sunny, the two little
Shetland mixed-breeds. Flip and Topper, and Flip's daughter, a little
black filly called Pennant, trotting at her side, following wherever
she went. Most of them were the solid black, long-maned, thick-
tailed beauties I soon learned were Fell ponies. I'd never seen this
breed before, and in all my eager research in the past I hadn't come
across them. But Mrs W. had explained on the drive yesterday that
Fell ponies were endemic to the north-west counties and, as their
name suggests, originated on the wide mountains and moorland
of Cumberland and Westmorland.

'Lovely animals!' Mrs W. said. 'They are small, but hardy, sure-
footed and patient: good-natured. Perfect for children learning to
ride.' This was why so many of her ponies were of this breed. That
first day, however, I found them hard to tell apart as I learned to
groom them: they were all black, and their manes were so long and
graceful they fell below their necks, and their forelocks reached
down over their noses.

Topper was an exception. He was a small grey pony, wiry and agile. Flip was the biggest of them all, an actual horse in fact, being taller than the requisite fifteen hands that makes a pony a horse. Flip was a crossbreed – Fell and Arab – and she was beautiful. She was a dark bay – brown with black points – and so elegant and yet sturdy. Mrs W. revealed to me her ambition: to one day buy an Arab stallion and breed more such beautiful Fell-Arab ponies, like Flip.

But for now, I had to be content with the little ones, mainly Lucky and Sunny, both geldings but two very different animals. Lucky, a chestnut, was a tad larger than Sunny, a heavy-set child-size pony and most friendly, always nudging for a snack. Sunny, however, was the unfriendliest of them all. Ears laid back, he was always ready to snap and nudge impatiently anyone who came near his head, or side-kick someone silly enough not to take a wide berth of his hindquarters. 'He's all right once you get on his back,' Mrs W. reassured me. But when would that be? For now, it was all about grooming, a thing I had, until now, only seen from afar at Georgetown's Mounted Branch, standing at the doors of the loose-boxes and stalls looking in enviously, never touching. Now, I could at last get up close and personal.

It started with hoof-picking. In patient, clear instructions Mrs W. taught me where to stand, how to coax a pony to lift its hooves one by one, how to hold the hooves and how to use a hoof-pick to clear out all the dried mud and caked grass within the hoof. With all the hooves picked clean, we moved on to the coat, working with a curry-comb, a hard brush and a body-brush. With their thick winter coats there was not much of a sleek shine to be expected, but nevertheless, each animal had to be thoroughly brushed and cleaned all over.

'They really enjoy it,' Mrs W. told me, 'and you should too.'

And I did. There was something mesmerising about the sound of the horses snatching mouthfuls of hay from the hay-nets, blissfully munching and crunching away, swishing their tails in contentment.

The very smell of them; their strong, muscular bodies; the gentle way they'd occasionally turn and nudge me while I worked: that made me the happiest little girl alive.

I soon got the knack of it. Over the coming days, once I could be trusted to work on my own, Mrs W. left me to do it all alone. Without her judging presence, I couldn't help but occasionally throw my arms around a pony's neck, nuzzle my face against its soft fur, press my cheek into its shoulder and inhale its fragrance, more delicious than any perfume. This was pony heaven, the place I'd dreamed of for years. I returned to the house for lunch exhilarated – and hungry.

Chapter Thirty-Six

Like a Boy

Dear Mum,

I love ponies more than humans. Maybe even more than you though I'll never tell you that. They know me and I know them. They are my real friends here. I love them with all my heart.

Sometimes I miss you but not always because my heart is filled with ponies.

Love Jo.

That first day there was more to be done, but not with horses. After lunch Mrs W. drove us to the nearby town of Millom. 'We need to get you some clothes,' she explained. I tried to figure out how to tell her I didn't want a dress, I wanted jodhpurs. My own, real, new jodhpurs, not somebody's hand-me-downs. It was, perhaps, the first time in my life, apart from my little food rebellions at school, that I'd be bluntly going against an adult's grain, contradicting their instruction and telling them I could not acquiesce in their decision. But I did it; once in the shop, she asked: 'So, Jo, what kind of home clothes would you like?' and I said it: 'Jodhpurs, please!'

Unfortunately, that was not to be. 'There's no point buying jodhpurs now,' she said. 'You won't be riding and you'll outgrow them by the time you will be riding, at Easter. But, if you like, maybe some nice trousers?'

I nodded eagerly.

The 'dress' question had been neatly avoided. But I couldn't help the sense of disquiet that now overtook me: no riding till Easter? Really? She had warned me earlier, true enough, but now that I was actually in among the ponies I panicked a little. Could I really wait that long? I was dying to get on the back of one of the lovely creatures I'd groomed that morning. If Mrs W. were Mummy, I'd beg and beg and badger to get her to change her mind. But I knew well that Mummy was special; I had no leverage to bend any other adult to my will. I had to do as I was told, like it or not. No riding until Easter.

For the time being, it was a whole new set of clothes for me. I chose a pair of tartan trousers and a green cardigan to match, and a few other items. It was then that Mrs W. came up with a brilliant idea.

'Jo,' she asked, 'have you considered what you'll give your mother for Christmas?'

I shook my head. Up to now all I'd ever done for Mum and Dad's presents was to draw pictures, mostly of horses. I had no idea what other presents I could give.

'What about a photograph?' she said. 'A photograph of you in your nice new clothes?'

I must have broken into a huge beaming smile, for she said, 'That's it, then. A lovely studio photo. If we do it now, it will get there in time.'

We went immediately to a Millom photographer to arrange for the photo. The photographer suggested that I go to a hairdresser first and return the next day. My hair, cut short before leaving for England back in September, had grown and become messy. I didn't really know what to do with it: I couldn't plait it myself, and anyway, it was still at that in-between stage, too short to plait, too long to keep neat, and at school there'd been no one to help me with it. I was in the habit of simply dragging a brush through it, grimacing when I encountered a tangle but not overly worried. Obviously, this was no style to please a professional photographer.

'We'll be back tomorrow,' Mrs W. told him, and ushered me off to her own hairdresser, who was able to fit me in immediately. Mrs W.'s own hair was as short as could be, in a rather masculine style; I was finding more and more areas of compatibility with her. When asked how I'd like my hair, I said simply, 'like a boy.' And it was done.

There could have been no prouder child in the whole of England as the next day, sporting my new haircut and my new tartan trousers and my new cardigan, I posed, hands stuck cheekily in my trouser pockets, for my new photo. This was the new me. I'd finally found my place in life.

Studio photo taken for Mum, winter 1961

'And what would *you* like for Christmas?' asked Mrs W. There could only ever be one answer to that, there had only ever been one answer: a book.

'Very well, I'll see to that,' said Mrs W. 'I know just the book.'

Meanwhile she took me to the library, registered me, and let me loose. And so, on top of pony heaven, there was book heaven. I knew I already had a whole bookshelf in my room at Summer Hill, but there could never be enough books. I made my choice and returned home with a heart swelling with joy.

To my intense disappointment, there really was no riding that season. The riding school did not open till the Easter holidays, said Mrs W. firmly, and I'd have to wait. She must have noticed how my face fell in disappointment, because she added, 'but Lynn is coming this weekend, and maybe she could give you a little lesson.'

Lynn was Mrs W.'s daughter, the younger one. But she wasn't a child, as I had hoped. She was an adult. The older daughter's name was Jonny, short for Jonquil, and she was married and lived further away. But Lynn lived just up the coast, in Seascale, and was engaged to be married to a cattle-farmer named David. She was a frequent visitor to Summer Hill, I was to find out, and in the warmer months she was her mother's right-hand woman with the riding school.

Lynn was quite impressive, even physically. I suspect that the absent Mr W. – I never found out if he was dead or divorced – must have been a very large man, for Mrs W. was quite short, agile and wiry, while Lynn was tall, strongly built, with, to me, a commanding presence. There was no monkeying around with her – not that it was my tendency to monkey around anyway, but even if I'd been tempted to slack off or be anything less than absolutely obedient and diligent – well, I wouldn't have dared. Not with Lynn. She was the kind of no-nonsense person who radiates authority. Lynn said the word, and you followed. Just what I needed.

Me with Lynn, cleaning tack outside the tack-room

And so, at last, I finally had my much-yearned for first riding lesson. My first time, ever, on horseback. *Properly* on horseback. As always with the W. family, it started with the basics: learning the parts of saddle and bridle – which I already knew in theory, having read up all about these matters – and how to bridle and saddle a pony. The victim was, obviously, the pony – Lucky, who stood patiently in the manège as Lynn demonstrated and then allowed me to try by myself. I learned how to ease the pony's mouth open, and slip the bit in and the bridle over the ears, how to gently fling the saddle over the back, where exactly to position it and how to tighten the girth to exactly the right degree of tautness, using two fingers.

That done, she taught me to mount, and I practised that for a while. And then there was the question of correct position: straight back, heels down, knees close to the saddle, reins threaded upwards through my fingers, fists upright. I learned the two inviolable Summer Hill riding rules: never kick your pony's sides, never pull the reins. '*Squeeze* with your calves!' Lynn taught me. '*Squeeze* the reins!'

Finally, I was allowed to move off. Around and around the manège I rode, Lucky patiently plodding beneath me. My first time on a pony's back gave me a new level of bliss, even if it was just walking around a manège instead of galloping over the endless hills, pony's mane and tail flying, me with one arm waving in new-found gleeful freedom. That was simply not to be. Not yet.

With the lesson over, Lucky had to be taken to the stable, unsaddled, unbridled, haltered, tied, given a hay-net and groomed again, after which I had to go back, tack-laden, to the tack-room. This was another inviolable Summer Hill rule: after every ride, the tack has to be thoroughly cleaned, emphasis on *thoroughly*. Lynn once again put me through my paces. The bridle had to be completely taken apart, then every little strap rubbed down with a rag soaked in ice-cold water until all the pony's grease was rubbed off, with particular attention being paid to the buckle bits. Same thing with the saddle and the stirrups' straps.

Once all the leather parts were cleaned with moist rags, they had to be nourished with saddle-soap to keep the leather supple. And then the bit and the stirrups had to be cleaned and polished. The whole process took longer than the actual ride, but that was Summer Hill for you. It was a set ritual of grooming the ponies, preparing their hay, feeding them, bringing them back and forth from the back field, caring for the tack as if it were precious silver, then mucking out the stalls and stables, carting horse droppings to the manure heap in a wheelbarrow and emptying it.

Finally, I was sent out into the fields with a wheelbarrow and a spade to collect all the piles of horse droppings from there and dump them too on said manure heap. Come rain or shine, with the blistering wind slapping my cheeks and cold numbing my bare hands – it turned out Mrs W. did not approve of gloves – I pushed my barrow until it grew full and heavy, ready for unloading. And so I was well and thoroughly inducted into what it meant to be a horse person. And it was hard work. While I'd never in my home life had to perform a single household chore, here at Summer Hill I was to make up for all those missed opportunities in a single winter. Yet I wouldn't have changed it for anything in the world. And, above all, I yearned for Easter, and summer, when my riding life would begin in earnest.

Chapter Thirty-Seven

The Most Depressing Christmas Ever

Dear Mum,

At last I got to sit on a pony's back! And I am with ponies all day, almost! But it is mostly work. I have to groom them, feed them, lead them back and forth between the stables and the fields, muck out the stables, muck out the fields, clean the tack, clean the tack-room. I don't know if I am having fun or not. It is quite cold and the house is cold apart from the kitchen. It is very windy in the morning and also dark when I go out to bring in the ponies. The wind is so strong I can hardly even stand up. I am afraid it will blow me away! I am so cold.

I sent you a Christmas present. I hope it comes in time. I hope you like it.

Love, Jo

Christmas came and went, and it was nothing like the joyous, warm, lively Christmases of my past. Back home in BG, Christmases were saturated with delightful smells and sounds, with coloured lights and Christmas trees in the windows, window-shopping, Santa Claus and an atmosphere to make your little heart race and your spirits soar.

Here at Summer Hill there was no Christmas tree, no blinking fairy-lights, no coloured streamers, no presents elaborately wrapped and bowed. For Christmas celebrations Mrs W. invited a few of her friends around as overnight house-guests. Lynn and her fiancé David came, as well as a lady called Joan – which was also Mrs W.'s Christian name – and a very funny man named Kanga, who may or may not have been Australian, and who told funny stories and sang funny songs. It was from beginning to end an adult affair with no concessions whatsoever to the only child in the house.

There was song-singing, but nothing Christmassy, and no carols at all. A firm favourite – then and in all the Summer Hill Christmases to come – was 'On Ilkley Moor Baht 'at'. Other rollicking songs were 'What Shall We Do With A Drunken Sailor?' and, for my benefit, perhaps, 'There's A Hole In My Bucket'.

Alcohol may have been involved in the festivities; certainly, the songs were accompanied by a lot of loud laughter and even, in some cases, dancing. Finding it all rather boring, I went to bed early. The next day, Christmas Day, Mrs W. finally paid tribute to the spirit of the occasion, and her own upbringing, by taking me to church in Bootle for the Christmas service. After that, Christmas dinner was served.

I did receive the books I'd requested, one from Mummy, and one from Mrs W. But there was none of the joyous unpacking of presents, like Christmas morning back home, none of the tearing off of coloured paper and ribbons, the oohs and aahs when the contents (for me, mostly books!) were revealed. None of the smells and sounds of Christmas, the radio playing 'Jingle Bells', the blinking lights; the friends and relatives in and out all day, all of us driving around town to visit each other. There was no joy at all. Even Mummy's book was a disappointment. The title was *My Friend Flicka*, and I started it that night. Mrs W. had told me she knew I'd love it, but I struggled with the first chapter and put it away for now. It was slow-moving, with lots of descriptive passages even in the first chapter, and adult conversations. Not my kind of book at all. Her own present was a book called *Hilda's Adventures*, which was about a New Zealand schoolgirl who had a horse. I did read that book over the next few days and loved it.

One important fact I grasped that first Christmas at Summer Hill was this: Brussels sprouts are as disgusting as peas. Fortunately, Mrs W. never put anything on my plate I didn't want, and allowed me to try new things via small portions. I did, however, like the roast turkey.

After Christmas, life at Summer Hill settled back to normal. The centre of the house was the kitchen, and the centre of the kitchen was the Aga, which kept everything deliciously warm. The rest of the house was virtually unheated; at least, my room was always cold. A hot-water bottle, filled from the constantly steaming kettle on the open Aga hotplate, made my bed the only refuge in my bedroom, and at night I'd snuggle and cuddle up until the bed itself grew warm. I'd read until I fell asleep. During the day, though, if I wasn't outside braving the weather I'd be in the kitchen, curled up, book in hand, on a comfy chair.

Mrs W.'s own private quarters were upstairs too, but on the other side of the house, accessed via a steep and narrow staircase leading up from the utility room. I was rarely invited up there, but when I was, I saw that it was a large, comfortably furnished room with carpeted floors, a cosy couch and a fireplace in which a fire roared.

Outside, of course, the wind raged and the skies stayed slate-grey, and although there was never any snow, winter made sure we knew our place. Bundled up in a warm jacket, cap and gloves, I'd emerge from the delicious Aga-warmth into the biting wind, into the cold wild darkness of early morning, and set about my morning duties. The worst of it all were my battles with the gate to the back field.

The wind was so strong, I could sometimes barely stand up against it, much less close a gate against it. It was a daily fight.

I'd always been a lover of the sea, and Summer Hill stood quite close to the cliff-edge. A gulley led down to the beach, and I went down a few times while exploring the region. But this wasn't a sea I could get close to. It was wild, icy cold and grey, forbidding rather than inviting, with waves whipped into fury by that angry wind.

'It's lovely in the summer!' Mrs W. comforted me. 'We sometimes go swimming with the horses.'

I was astonished. 'How?'

'Bareback,' she said. 'The horses swim, and the riders cling to their manes. It's lovely.'

I could not imagine ever being confident enough on a horse's back to go swimming in that angry sea on it, but summer was something to look forward to. I was quite aware that this winter was not a typical Summer Hill experience. I yearned for summer, for sunshine, and a proper beach and proper sea, which in my mind should be soft, warm and transparent, like the aquamarine sea of Barbados, St Lucia or Tobago. Even the Atlantic Ocean lapping the Georgetown seafront was more welcoming than this. Brown water, maybe, but gentle, and above all, *warm.*

I longed for sunshine. I was cold. I yearned for home. For people I knew. For Mummy's arms, her smile, her stories at night. I longed for Daddy and his jokes, the smell of his car as he drove me back and forth between his home and mine, the chaos and noise of Crown Street, Uncle Denis and his antics. I longed for Granny's soft lap, and for hooking into Aunt Leila's elbow as we crossed the streets to walk to the market or the Sea Wall. This wild, bleak landscape brought into stark relief all the delights of home. I missed it all, but I was far, far away. For the time being, I'd have to make do with ponies. After all, that was what I'd wanted.

Chapter Thirty-Eight

Easter Term

In a wink those dreary Christmas holidays were over. Mrs W. drove me back to school, making the obligatory jokes about Wigglesworth and Gigglewick. All reverted to the new normal.

This term I found myself in a dorm called Top Ten. It was in a wing of its own, and opposite was a room called Top Five. Down a staircase were the corresponding dorms Bottom Ten and Bottom Five. The numbers corresponded to the number of beds. Over my time at Oakdale, I was to be assigned to each one of these dorms in turn. Each had their own benefits and disadvantages, but over them all reigned the terrifying Miss Dare, the head matron. Miss Almond still took care of our day-to-day needs. Her nickname of Mummy Almond was well earned; she was quintessentially motherly, kind-hearted yet no-nonsense in nature, her favourite admonishment being *chop-chop girls, no dawdling!* She bustled about between the two floors, making sure we were all ready in time for the day or, at night, kneeling at our bedsides saying our prayers until the final Lights Out.

Lights Out, for us, was when the fun began. Once Mummy Almond closed the door on us, the whispering and giggling would begin, growing louder and more bold the later the night grew. We could not be stopped. There may have been a few good girls who wanted to sleep, and did, but I was not one of them. I laughed and chattered as much as the rest. I loved it best when I shared a room with Jackie, who was funnier and more creatively mischievous than all the others. It was she, after all, who'd write a play about St Trinian's a year later, and it was under her influence that a mischievous streak began to sprout in me, most especially after Lights Out.

Talking or playing after Lights Out could earn you an Order Mark if you were caught by Mummy Almond. Worse yet: Miss Dare might throw open the door, flick the light switch and catch you red-handed in the glaring light. If you'd done something really naughty, you'd get a Report.

A favourite game was dares, and as time and terms went on, the dares grew bolder. They mostly involved sneaking out of the room to go either upstairs or downstairs to visit another dorm. In time, a particularly bold dare became running a bath and getting into it. Then, it was taking off your pyjama top or bottom and running down the corridor half-naked.

That was how, one dreadful night, I was caught. I'd been dared to visit another dorm without my pyjama bottoms. Just as I was about to run back to my old dorm, a white-clothed, red-faced Miss Dare suddenly appeared in the doorway.

'Jo! Where on earth are your pyjama trousers!' she bellowed.

I sheepishly looked down and, pretending I had noticed for the first time that something was missing, I squeaked, 'I don't know, Miss Dare!'

And so I earned, for the first and last time, a Report. Three of those and I'd be reading out at assembly. I made sure that I was never again caught. My emerging mischievousness had to be kept securely under wraps. To the mistresses, I was a well-behaved and industrious pupil. By the end of that Easter term I'd earned my first green deportment badge.

With only one bathroom on each floor, we certainly had to move quickly, bending over the washbasins for face-washing and teeth-cleaning with a queue of impatient girls waiting their turn. Each bathroom had several sinks and a bathtub. Baths were three times a week, either Monday–Wednesday–Friday or Tuesday–Thursday–Saturday, in about six inches of water – no leisurely soaking. Hair-washing was Wednesday afternoon, in lieu of games.

Every day though, we had the Morning Run, with some senior girl calling out what we were to wear. As the weather improved we moved from macs-caps-and-wellingtons to macs-and-game-shoes, ending up, by the end of term, with just game-shoes. Though I was never much good at sports, I loved gymnastics. It was one of my favourite subjects. I wasn't particularly good at it, but I loved it nevertheless. Some girls were brilliant: they leapt over the buck and the horse with ease. I preferred climbing: rope climbing, or up the wooden frame at the back of the gym. But I'll never forget the day one girl had a very bad fall.

The girl was Rosemary, and she was from Singapore. She was a petite girl, light as a fairy, and while springing over the buck she fell and broke her arm. There she sat in the middle of the floor holding up her left arm, which had a distinct U-bend in the middle of it. It was horrific. While Rosemary, tended by Matron, waited for the ambulance, we were all shooed to one end of the gym and eventually taken out, but we'd seen it already. That U-bend in an arm that should have been straight. It's one of those indelible images that carve themselves into the mind of a ten-year-old.

Oakdale took good care of every aspect of our lives. One of the 'extras' was a matter called Remedials, for which some of us were called up, including me. My remedial was posture, and I suppose the treatment I was given would be called physiotherapy today. I had a tendency to slouch, but it was fixed so well that I earned my second – red – deportment badge, for which a straight back was one of the criteria, by the end of the summer term. In my second year, I won the coveted blue Deportment girdle.

Another Remedial was flat feet, and another was speech. I should probably have been given speech Remedials but, quite possibly due to the fact that I spoke so little, it escaped the teachers' notice that I had a disability. Or maybe I just spoke so slowly and carefully that I managed to keep it hidden. But we also had diction classes, and that helped.

For diction, we learned to speak clearly, distinctly and with feeling so we could recite poems in chorus. These were mostly the poems of Edward Lear: *They went to sea in a sieve, they did, in a sieve they went to sea!* And: *Far and few, far and few, are the lands where the Jumblies live.*

Quite often, there were diction competitions with other schools. Our greatest competitor, in diction as well as in sports and music, was Queen Ethelburga's, a girls' school not far away. Our diction mistress was an older woman called Miss Rutherford, who had the kind of cut-glass voice that was, apparently, the thing to aspire to. I knew from the start I'd never speak like that, nor did I want to.

Back in BG, I had been coached by most of my elders to 'speak properly', that is, not to resort to the kind of 'broken English' that constitutes the dialect known as Creolese, a home-grown vernacular that rejoices in using the present tense for past, willy-nilly replacing *I* with *me* and vice versa, or simply abbreviating words: *whu* for what and so on, all spoken with a distinctive Guyanese rhythm. Each Caribbean country has its own version of Creole, and ours has a music of its own.

In Miss Rutherford's diction class the aim was to achieve a uniquely upper-class British accent, but that was not something I strove for. There had to be a compromise between raw Creolese and 'talking posh', or, more exactly for a middle-class brown-skinned girl, 'talking white', which back home was likely to earn you jibes for pretending to be above your station. This was not a good thing, and I sensed it even as a child.

However, learning to methodically speak with cut-glass clarity helped me in another way. It was a chance to overcome that speech impediment I was so ashamed of. I was still – quite literally –

tongue-tied, and reluctant to let my voice be heard, at least by adults, but in those diction classes I learned to speak slowly and meticulously, avoiding the slurred, muffled speech I was so ashamed of. Diction with Miss Rutherford did the job admirably. I found my middle way: a version of the Queen's English that did not sound affected, had a slight Guyanese lilt, and was correct, if slow and sometimes slurred. But I never got over my self-consciousness about public speaking, or, for that matter, speaking at all. The effort needed to speak clearly slowed down my mental processes; I always found it far more difficult to put my thoughts on a subject into spoken words than written ones.

Chapter Thirty-Nine

Rising to the Trot

We all had to learn a musical instrument. Our 'musicality' was individually tested and the girls rated 'musical' were allowed to learn the violin. I turned out to be non-musical and therefore was put in the 'less-musical' recorder group.

But I liked the recorder, and soon our beginners' class was competing with our main rival Queen Ethelburga's, and other schools. These were competitions with external judges. Sometimes we won, sometimes we didn't. Sometimes we squeaked out of tune.

But for music, too, I had an impediment: that broken hand. The bones had never slotted back into place. One bone between my index finger and thumb stuck out, and the finger was unable to bend down at the joint. As a result, it could not properly cover some of the recorder's holes. It was the same with every instrument I ever tried. I could never have played the violin, even if I'd wanted to, because I could not reach the first string; and it was the same, later, with the guitar.

But I loved music. There was one girl, in particular, who played the piano beautifully. Her name was Elizabeth and, unusually, she came from Montevideo in Uruguay – another South American country. How I wished I could play an instrument too; and the piano seemed easier than the violin – which I wasn't allowed to play – yet more sophisticated than the recorder. So I wrote to Mum with a request to learn the piano, which would involve extra, private lessons. My wish was soon granted.

But here too I was disabled: my index finger was useless, so I could only play with three fingers and the thumb of my left hand. Anything that involved the left index finger meant trouble. Still, I somehow managed, and eventually advanced up to Grade Two, after which I dropped the piano entirely. I concluded that they were all right; I just wasn't musical, and couldn't learn an instrument.

But what about singing? Wasn't that a possibility? I wouldn't need that finger at all for singing. I'd always yearned for, but never came close to, a beautiful singing voice. I couldn't hold a tune for the life of me – and anyway, singing would involve my voice, which I hated. I'd never have sung in public.

The Easter term came to an end and once again Mrs W. came to pick me up. This time I knew what I was heading for, and my excitement was boundless, because the riding school would be open. Finally!

I still had to rein in my expectations. There was no galloping across the green hills of Cumberland. Round and round the manège we all rode at a walk, I and the four or five girls – it was almost always girls – in the beginners' class. Either Lynn or Mrs W. herself took these classes and, as always, it was the basics first: mounting and dismounting, straight back, alignment of heel, hip, shoulder and ear, head up and hands relaxed around the reins. Stopping and starting, turning and talking, communicating silently through the reins. That was a language I could speak. It was all a matter of relaxing into the horse's gait, feeling a oneness with its motion and directing it through the slightest squeeze of the reins – never pulling! Thighs, calves, heels, hands, eyes, voice: every part of the body had a role to play, and *always*, it was sensitivity that counted. I had that in spades. As did Lynn.

Lynn, a woman who by appearance alone – big and strong – seemed the very antithesis of sensitive, in fact possessed the very essence of that deep synthesis of understanding and gentleness needed as the foundation for fusion between rider and horse. And her goal, in those first lessons, was to impart that sense of innate communication to us beginners. At last I had found something, a *physical* something, that fell into my lap with ease. I was created for riding, I found. This was it. The epitome of my reason for being: to become one. With a pony.

It very soon emerged that Topper, the little grey, was my favourite. Topper was light-footed and slightly flighty. I had the feeling that he was impatient with the endless circles round and round the manège, as we beginners straightened our backs and raised our chins and stopped flapping our elbows and closed the gaps between knees and saddle. He was slightly skittish, in fact, but I loved that skittishness. It challenged me, and once we learned to trot, I knew I'd found my life-partner.

Of course 'rising to the trot' was the next hurdle, but I soon mastered it, followed by the canter. Again, we rode endless circles around the manège until we were all at ease in every gait. Only then did Lynn take us out for rides over the fields, down the lanes and even down to the beach. It was all glorious.

All too soon it was back to Harrogate for the summer term. 'Wait until you return for the summer holidays,' Mrs W. promised as she bade me goodbye. 'There'll be Pony Club rallies and events – maybe you'll even be good enough to compete! And treks! And swimming on horseback!'

I could hardly wait. But first, I had the summer term to navigate.

Summer term meant free time. We could go out into the sunshine, wander around the grounds and lie in the sun. Most importantly, we were allowed small pets: hamsters, guinea pigs and little white mice, kept in the pet-shed. We were allowed to look after them every afternoon: feed them, clean their cages and play with them on the grass. I did not have a pet, but Carole's parents bought her a hamster that she shared with me, which was a huge source of delight and fun; a little creature we could bond over. We took turns to feed it every day, and on Saturdays and Sundays we'd take it out of its cage and let it run on the grass. It wasn't exactly a pony, but I gave that little creature all I had.

Our weekdays were filled with lessons and sport – swimming, tennis, athletics or rounders – and, it seemed, we were to be educated even on Saturdays and Sundays. We'd usually be lined up to troop down to the gym to listen to some lecturer, who was always some man or other who had brought along his collection of slides with which he would illustrate some particularly boring trip he had made to the Outer Hebrides or wherever. I'm sure the trips these lecturers made weren't boring, but describing them to a gym-full of prepubescent girls longing to go out into the sunshine – well, nothing could have been more sleep-inducing, and I never retained a single word or a single image of those lectures.

Sometimes, though, we went on excursions, and foremost among these was the trip to the Brontë Parsonage Museum – to us, simply the Brontë house. We'd not yet read any of the Brontë sisters' novels, but it was a trip into the past, to a place caught in a time-bubble where we could actually imagine real people in that house, sitting in the chairs, reading and writing books. To me, at least, it stirred the imagination and made me wonder about the things I'd always wondered about: life and death, the meaning of it all, and God.

We went to the Mystery Plays in York, and stately houses of historical interest in the vicinity – all soon forgotten. We went to a production of Gilbert and Sullivan's *The Mikado*, and for weeks afterwards we were all singing 'Three Little Maids from School Are We' and acting out the lyrics of 'Behold! The Lord High Executioner!' That trip must have inspired my friend Jackie, who went on to write and direct a play of her own, based on the famous fictional boarding school St Trinian's. The theme song to that play went something like this: 'We are the girls of St Trinian's, not little angels but little sinnians...'

Jackie offered me a role in her play but I refused. I was far, far too shy. How could I possibly stand onstage and speak the part out loud! I'd have sunk through the floorboards. But I loved the play and laughed until I got a stitch in my tummy.

Then it was the summer holidays again. I went back to Summer Hill – now my official home – and as the child-in-residence I held a certain status. Other children came and went; they stayed for a week or two. They came from all over England, Scotland, and even America.

One little girl told me, the moment she arrived, 'My name is Mary-Sue and I'm from Boston. Have you ever heard of Boston? Have you ever heard of the Boston Tea Party?' I hadn't, and it would be years before I knew what that was, but this was the way she greeted every new person. We did become good friends for the time she stayed, and, like every other child who came, she cried when she left.

'You're so lucky!' they'd weep. 'You get to stay here all the time! I don't want to go home!' And I knew that for once, I was the privileged one.

As Mrs W. had promised, I joined the local branch of the Pony Club, and a new pony-filled world opened up to me. On Saturdays we'd all troop off, on horseback, across the fields to Bootle or wherever this weekend's event was to be held.

By now I was quite a competent little rider, and at these events and rallies I progressed even further. At home I'd started jumping and the prospect was held out to me that soon, very soon, I could compete. I began to learn the rudiments of dressage as well. I wasn't yet good enough to compete, but that was also a carrot held out to me. Maybe next year?

Nothing was more exciting than a three-day event, one day dedicated to each discipline of dressage, cross-country riding and showjumping, and though I couldn't yet compete, Lynn did, and always took home a prize ribbon or two. It was the most exciting thing in the world, and I couldn't wait to participate instead of standing on the sidelines and applauding Lynn's wins.

Sometimes we went on cross-country treks, or even on overnight camping trips, sleeping in our tents. Mrs W. would join us, driving to the campsite in Frances the station-wagon, bringing sausages to roast over an open fire. As promised, sometimes we went swimming on horseback, and nothing was more exhilarating than a pony plunging through the waves while you hung on to its mane or hugged its neck, screaming with joy, clinging on for dear life.

But it wasn't all fun and games; all the children had to help with the grooming of the ponies, the mucking-out of the stables, and the cleaning of the tack. There was never an excuse, and always an inspection. Some of the posher children might have complained, but not one could escape. Lynn and Mrs W. were both hard taskmasters.

On Sundays we all rode to church, across fields full of scampering rabbits and grazing sheep, in and out of gates, clattering down the road and filing into the little church to fill the back pews.

In all this time, it never once occurred to me that I stuck out like a sore thumb. Not being able to see myself from the outside – except for my hands and arms – I didn't really view myself as different to the others, my face a single brown blob amid all the white ones. This was a rural, very conservative area; most of the community had most likely never seen a living dark-skinned person in their lives, and may have had very vivid imaginations as to what we foreigners were like – and would certainly have had their prejudices.

Was I treated differently? Was I looked at askance? I didn't know. I was enjoying myself far too much to notice. I got on well with the child guests, and I didn't care what the adults thought. But looking back, I do wonder. Did they look with curiosity at the little brown girl in Mrs W.'s care? And what did it matter? I was in seventh heaven, living the life I'd always wanted, on the backs of ponies. All memory of home, of BG, of Mummy and the backyard, faded away. This was the life.

The summer was over far too quickly, and it was back to school. On the long drive there, Mrs W. turned to me.

'Jo,' she said, 'why don't you call me Aunty Joan from now on?'

Not revealing my shock, I replied, 'All right.' But inside me I knew this could never be. Mrs W. was not my aunty. Aunties were those warm and caring women I'd grown up with, smelling of Johnson's Baby Powder and Limacol. Whether they were related to me or not, they were women who wrapped you in warmth and love and made you feel you belonged.

Our mutual love of horses may have made Mrs W. and me soulmates of a kind, but it could not pierce the membrane that enclosed the silent realms of my heart. Outside the unique world of ponies and horses, of tack and saddle-soap, of hay-nets and dungheaps, we remained virtual strangers.

When we arrived at school, she hugged me goodbye as usual. 'Goodbye, Jo! See you next holidays!'

'Goodbye,' I replied. She hesitated, waiting for that confirming 'Aunty Joan'. It never came, then or thereafter, though my letters home did politely address her as such.

Chapter Forty

The Chocolate Bar Thief

My darling Jo,

I have such exciting news: I am coming to England! I will be visiting you at school in June. I look forward to seeing you again with all my heart! I'm counting the days!

All my love,
Mum

My second and final year at Oakdale began. It was the year that I finally earned my blue girdle for deportment. It was also the year I discovered I wasn't that bad at lacrosse, and actually pretty good at long jump, winning second place on Sports Day. And it was the year when, in the summer term 1963, I killed a hamster, and was accused of being a thief.

One day a rumour spread: a girl was missing a chocolate bar, and somebody must have stolen it. With the speed of light, the Mystery of the Stolen Chocolate Bar became a whodunnit of massive proportions, not only among the girls, but among the staff too. The culprit had to be found.

We were interviewed, one by one, as if we were all suspects in this crime to end all crimes. Then we were told to sit in little groups in the front hall and discuss the matter, to see if we could get the thief to finally confess. We were told to report any suspicions to staff.

To my surprise, I was called to Killer's office. It was the only time, ever, I had been called there; it was something that only really naughty girls were subject to. Shaking with trepidation, I knocked on the door.

'Enter!' said the voice from within.

Killer sat behind her huge desk, Miss Dare at her side. I was not invited to sit.

'Jo,' she said, not unkindly, but sternly.

'Yes, Miss Killingley,' I managed to squeak.

'You know we are trying to find out who took Jane's chocolate bar. I'm afraid your name has emerged as one of the chief suspects.'

My shyness vanished in a flash. 'Me? No! I didn't! I didn't, I didn't!' I cried, and burst into tears.

Killer and Miss Dare exchanged a glance. Finally, Miss Dare emerged from behind the desk.

'There, there, dear, don't cry. We're not saying you did it.'

'But we had to investigate!' said Killer, in a soothing voice.

'I didn't! I really didn't!' I sobbed, somewhat mollified. How could I prove my innocence? Did they believe me, or did they believe my accuser? And who would do such a thing, accuse me, when I didn't do it? The only girls I could think of who disliked me enough to do such a thing were the Gwens.

I sniffled. 'I really didn't!' I continued to sob.

They both smiled, as if finally convinced. Killer stood up and came around from behind her desk. She patted me on the shoulder, bent down and kissed me on the cheek.

'We believe you, dear. Please don't cry. Now return to your classroom, you don't want to miss anything.'

If being accused by some anonymous enemy as a thief had shocked me, a kiss from Killer almost eviscerated me. It was the kiss to end all kisses.

A few days later the missing chocolate bar turned up in a corner of the victim's locker, and the mountain turned back into a molehill, or rather, disappeared in a cloud of vapour. Poof! I earned a few minutes of fame by letting it be known that Killer had kissed me. Not one of the other girls could make such a claim.

As for killing the hamster: this happened later in the same term. Once again, I was sharing a hamster with Carole. She went out on an exeat one Saturday, leaving the poor hamster in my care. I was playing with him outside, letting him run on the grass, when along came Penny, a big strong sporty girl, who I believe was the captain of the lacrosse team, bounding across the field. It was over in less than a second. Splat! Poor little hamster, squashed flat under Penny's foot.

We were *all* hysterical: myself, Penny, all the girls who'd witnessed it – poor little hamster, just his forequarters squashed, his hind legs still wriggling! We were weeping and wailing, being comforted by the mistresses. I dreaded Carole's return, and having to break the devastating news to her. Needless to say, she was weeping and wailing too.

Carole's parents bought her a new hamster. She shared it with Penny. I was out of the picture from then on, our friendship at an end. She had obviously decided that it was me, not Penny, who had killed the hamster, and I was to be punished and Penny comforted. I was devastated, and nobody knew. I swallowed the guilt and shame. But the memory of that poor hamster's wiggling hindquarters haunted me for years afterwards. I never told a soul.

On Sunday evenings we were allowed to watch television, sitting either cross-legged on the floor or on chairs in the main assembly hall. Over several sessions in April and May of 1963, we gathered to watch the six-part BBC series *Jane Eyre*. We loved it. We were on the edge of our seats, held spellbound by the little screen as the poor residents of Thornfield Hall were beleaguered by the madwoman in the attic. None of us had yet read the book, of course. That was waiting for us at senior school, and so we watched as innocents, not knowing the end.

The madwoman, we all soon realised, was Grace Poole. For weeks on end, that name became a synonym for rabid, lethal insanity. We'd play games after Lights Out, with someone pretending to be her on a rampage: 'I am Grace Poole!' we'd say in a spooky, wavering voice, 'Escaped from my attic prison!'

But then, towards the end of the series and in a final twist we hadn't seen coming, poor Grace Poole was redeemed. We'd been completely bamboozled by an ingenious red herring, our emotions stirred into a frenzy of false accusations and fear. We were shocked into a truth that was even more horrendous: Grace Poole was innocent! She was *good*! There was a *real* madwoman in the attic and she was downright *dangerous*!

Once again, I was unconsciously made aware of the power of storytelling. Whether a story came through words (books) or acting (films), it could sweep you up into a different world and convince you, for a window of time, that it was all real life, really happening in real time. Such is the power of the pen.

Then, right in the middle of the summer term, Mum came to visit. She took me out on exeat. Surely she'd planned a joyous reunion, and perhaps had had ideas for spending half-term or longer with me? But it was all a huge flop. In fact, it was a disaster.

When she picked me up at school, I was sullen and rude, rebuffed her hug, and didn't greet her. When she took me to lunch at a restaurant – not the Old Swan – I refused to speak to her. She asked me questions, and I didn't answer. I wouldn't meet her eyes. I didn't ask any questions – about Granny or Aunt Leila or Home – and when she tried to make conversation, I refused to listen, and made a bored face. I was, in fact, the very image of a spoilt, obnoxious, ungrateful little brat. And to top it all off, at the end of the meal I demanded to be returned to school.

'Don't come back!' I told her. 'Go home.'

Poor Mum. She took my rudeness and rebuffs stoically. Not a word of rebuke – which I would have deserved – not a word of disappointment, not even a tear. Perhaps she cried when she returned to her hotel, but I'd never know that. Mum kept her feelings to herself, always, just like I did. She simply swallowed them. What else was she to do? I sent her away, and she went without another word. And she didn't come back. She didn't try again.

Only later did I realise how devastatingly heartbreaking this reaction of mine must have been to her. I felt so terribly guilty afterwards, and later I did apologise, fleetingly, in a letter. But over time, the guilt began to grow. How could I do that to her? What a terrible, awful, ungrateful person I was! *What is wrong with me?* I'd ask myself again and again. I didn't know; I just knew there *was* something inherently, deeply wrong. And I had no idea how to put it right. Even years later, I could never think back to that disastrous visit without a deep sense of guilt, self-recrimination and remorse. Not even now. It was an echo of the incident at the London Zoo, when I wouldn't let her sit with me on the elephant, only much, much worse.

Chapter Forty-One

The Facts of Life

Dear Mum,

*Thank you for the long letter telling me the Facts of Life.
I didn't really want to know but I know anyway. Miss B.
the junior matron told us.*

Love, Jo

This was the year that a young woman, I'll call her Miss B.,
joined the Oakdale staff. I'm not sure of her role: was she an
assistant matron, or an intern, or on work experience? Either
way, she couldn't have been long out of school herself, and
was very much on our side. By now we were all getting rather
curious about something: that adult thing they were all so coy
about, deceptively and euphemistically called the Facts of Life.
Nobody really knew very much, but we'd look up hilarious
words in the dictionary, underline them and giggle – words like
'breast' and 'penis'.

Miss B. was very friendly and forthcoming and answered many
of our questions. And then, she smuggled a forbidden novel into
the dorm. It was a very naughty book, she told us, with lots of
naughty words, and we'd better hide it. And if it were ever found
please, please, please don't tell on her, for it could get her sacked.

That book was a goldmine of information. It was a romantic novel, and it contained scenes of an appallingly lewd nature: scenes with men and women *kissing*, and wandering hands, and heaving breasts, and smouldering glances. We were all very impressed and took care to keep the book hidden under a floorboard. This was a step up from the dictionary. We underlined whole passages of a risqué nature, and felt very adult indeed. A rumour spread that in the first year in Lower Fourth at senior school we'd be given a talk on this whole mysterious matter by the headmistress. We couldn't wait.

This was also the year when we'd be gradually prepared for entering senior school, and over the months our excitement grew. The main thing for us was choosing our house. Girls at Harrogate Ladies' College were physically separated by their houses – there were eight of them – where they slept and with which they identified. York and Lancaster were school houses, meaning they occupied two floors of the main school premises on Clarence Drive. Their colours were, respectively, light green and red . Swinton House was a lovely ivy-covered house, and its colour was orange, but it was undesirable because it was some distance from school, and so meant a daily trudging back and forth. Balliol House was the next furthest, down Clarence Drive from school, and its colour was purple. Armaclare, yellow, was just across the road from school.

At the perfect distance, not too far and not too near, and with no road to cross, was Lincoln. There were two Lincolns: Lincoln East and Lincoln West. Lincoln's colour was blue – dark blue for East and light blue for West – and it was housed in another beautiful manor-like building just down the road from school, but accessed through the school grounds and so a comfortable walk between the other school buildings.

Girls who had an older sister in one of the houses were automatically assigned to their sister's house. The rest of us could choose. And somehow it emerged that Lincoln was the hippest house to be in, not only distance-wise but size-wise and colour-wise. Could there be a hipper colour than blue? Blue, to my young mind, was the colour of boys and adventure and courage, of being the opposite of a sissy girl who played with dolls. And it seemed that many of my classmates agreed with me, because Lincoln was the first choice for most of us without big sisters.

But that year a new option came into play. Clarence House would be opening in 1963, another lovely building located between Lincoln and school. Its colour was pink. Nobody put down Clarence as her first choice. If Lincoln was the hippest, Clarence was the sissiest.

Unfortunately, though, some of us *had* to be assigned to Clarence, an empty house in need of filling. These girls were randomly selected – names out of a hat perhaps – and the decision was final.

The day came, towards the end of the summer term 1963, when we were informed of our house assignments. The list of Clarence girls was read out to gasps of horror. Had they been told they were about to be sent off to a gulag in Siberia, the dismay could not have been greater. Girls broke down in fits of shock, sobbing and blubbering. Was it the fact that it was a new house, a house without tradition or history? Or was it the colour pink? I suspect the latter.

To my great relief, I was assigned to Lincoln West. My colour would be blue. Light blue, to be sure, infinitesimally less hip than the dark blue of Lincoln East, but Lincoln nonetheless. The hippest house of them all. I couldn't wait.

As the term folded into its second half, we school leavers began to plot. We had to have a midnight feast, and it had to be on the very last night of term. I was beside myself with excitement: this was the stuff of legend. What could be more essential to this whole English boarding school experience than a real-life forbidden midnight feast! Surely it was the quintessential cloak-and-dagger event in the life of any self-respecting boarding-school girl? It certainly was according to Enid Blyton, the writer who had lured me here with her captivating stories of St Clare's and Malory Towers. A real, true midnight feast would be the most fitting end to our Oakdale years. And it would be the biggest feast ever, one that would go down in history.

We planned it thoroughly. This would be a feast to end all feasts. The whole year group would be involved, and for reasons of space we wouldn't hold it in one of the dorms but in the gym. All girls going out on half-term and exeats were instructed to bring back as much in the way of provisions as they could. Those of us who stayed behind were told to save our tuck and hide it. This we all did.

On the big night, loaded with Mars Bars and Crunchies and gobstoppers as well as sausage rolls, scones and Yorkshire puddings salvaged from exeats a few weeks previously, we padded silently down the stairs in our dressing gowns and slippers, smothering our giggles and shushing each other sternly. We made it down safely.

In the middle of the gym floor we laid out all the goodies, and soon we were all tucking in, stuffing our mouths with a strange array of our long-hoarded treats. And now, freed of the need for secrecy, we giggled and chattered as we gobbled.

But then: *bang bang bang!* Three mind-chilling knocks on the locked gym door! In horror, we looked at each other. The knocks came again. One of us managed to pull herself out of her shocked trance and pad up to the door and open it. There, her face beetroot-red with rage, stood Miss Dare.

'What on earth are you all doing?' she bellowed. Stunned into silence, we all just stared. Miss Dare in her dressing gown might be slightly less scary than Miss Dare in full matronly uniform, but she was still terrifying enough. She bellowed orders to gather up the remains of our picnic and bring them with us. Petrified, we obeyed, trooping up the stairs again. Convicts about to be shot couldn't have been more terrified.

Miss Dare herded us into a corridor at some distance from our dorms and told us to sit and wait. We waited in silence, cross-legged against the corridor walls, exchanging frantic glances, mouthing secret messages, not daring to say a word aloud – the very walls might be listening. After an eternity, Miss Dare returned with Killer in tow, also in her dressing gown.

Killer walked up and down between the rows of silent girls, looking down at us with furious censure as we sat, frozen with fear, lined up along the corridor. She was followed by arms-crossed Miss Dare, staring daggers down at us. The two then disappeared. Another eternity passed while we looked at each other in terror and mouthed more secret messages.

Finally, the two dragons reappeared. A furious tirade ensued, and our punishment was disclosed.

'You will all be having the remains of that feast for breakfast!' Killer announced in her most terrifying voice.

Our sentence announced, we were herded back to our dorms. As soon as the door closed on us, we broke into uncontrolled giggles. The best punishment *ever*!

Sadly for Killer and her right-hand woman, there was little they could do to punish us on the very day we were to go home forever. A breakfast clearing-up of the remains was the worst punishment they could devise. For us, though, the best.

And so it happened. The breakfast tables for the Upper Third next morning consisted of all the left-over sausage rolls, Milky Ways, roly-poly pudding and rock-hard scones, some of them several weeks old. It seemed, though, that Killer and Miss Dare were overcome with a guilty conscience about making us eat food that was old and possibly spoilt and mouldy; after breakfast we were herded into the front hall and each of us given a spoonful of castor oil. It was the vilest thing that has ever passed my lips. Worse, even, than liver. And *that* was the real punishment.

Chapter Forty-Two

Dressage

Dear Mum,

I'm back at Summer Hill, and Lynn says I'm good enough to start training for a Pony Club three-day event in late summer! I'm going to be riding Topper! My favourite pony!

Love, Jo

That summer, I finally became a rider who had earned her spurs.

'How would you like to take part in a three-day event?' asked Lynn. I gave a little leap of joy. She smiled. 'It will mean a lot of practice! You can ride Topper.'

Topper, of course, was the icing on the cake. But Lynn was right; it meant hard work. Unlike the other young competitors, I'd only been riding for a year. I had a lot to catch up. That meant extra lessons in dressage and showjumping, both of which I loved, and both of which required utter discipline and perfect communication between me and my pony. The cross-country competition, on the other hand, meant the fulfilment of a dream: galloping over the open fields, leaping over low barriers and streams, and I threw myself into practice.

Dressage meant, first of all, perfecting my seat. It meant maintaining a ramrod-straight yet supple back through every motion of the pony, a back that moved with the pony's movement but remained in position, with hips relaxed enough to perfectly adapt to the motion beneath. Discipline in riding can never be rigid, Lynn told me, it must flow, combining absolute concentration on the correct moves with hair-thin sensitivity to the pony as well as to my own body. Hips, thighs, calves, hands, elbows, heels and head all working together. But it all starts with a mental practice, an attitude of mind, a question of tact and feel. 'You'll need patience, compassion, repetition and understanding for Topper,' said Lynn. 'You have to become one with him.'

I wanted nothing more. Nothing, no English or French exam, had ever challenged me this much. I'd never felt so on top of the world as now, in learning how to ride. It meant fine-tuning my mind so as to become acutely sensitive to my mount, to speak without words. Perfect rapport, unity. Perfect communication, without words: it was the height of all the skills I'd ever master.

And on Topper, my favourite pony! I actually loved Flip the most, the gentle and beautiful bay mare. But Flip was much too big for me – or I was much too small for her. She was far out of my league. Hopefully I'd grow, and one day would be able to ride, and even compete on, Flip. Meanwhile Flip's little daughter, Pennant, was now a two-year-old, and almost ready to be broken in. Mrs W. had said I could help.

I started my dressage training and soon I knew the sequence by heart. I practised all through that summer, and simultaneously learned showjumping. I was determined to be a worthy representative of Summer Hill at the three-day event. It was the first time, ever, that I had worked towards a particular goal – apart from the obligatory school exams – and I put heart and soul into it.

In the meantime, children came and went as usual to learn to ride or develop their riding skills. Even more than last year, I was now an established part of Summer Hill. I could fling myself onto the bare back of a pony and swim with it in the sea without fear of falling. I still loved every aspect of pony care and riding, and I still hated tack-cleaning, although by now I'd accepted it had to be done. The perfect bridle was one that was black and supple with age, as flexible as rubber, and that only came with care. Nobody liked a new bridle, stiff and yellow.

Over the summer we once again went to several Pony Club rallies and events. One person stood out at all these gatherings: a tall, grey-haired man referred to as The Commander. The Commander, who was presumably a Second World War veteran, had, true to his nickname, an unbelievably commanding presence. Always immaculate in jodhpurs and jacket, he was one of those people who even without speaking a word transmitted a sense of authority, though I suppose having a title like The Commander was enough for that trick. He never actually commanded anyone but he was an impressive presence at every Pony Club meeting: tall, straight and imposing, rarely speaking. He had a long face, rather pink. He rode a big dun gelding, and I believe in the one photo of me at one of these events that dun gelding can be seen in the background.

At last, the big day arrived. Lynn drove the competing ponies over to the Bootle showground in a horsebox, with me beside her in the cabin. Lynn was going to compete in one of the adult events, but I felt, I *knew*, she was just as excited for me.

There were, of course, several levels of competition, and I was in the under-12s group. One by one the young riders were called up, and finally my name and number were called.

I was ready and waiting, with my competition number tied prominently to my back. I walked into the dressage manège, sedate and confident on Topper's back. I stopped, bowed to the judges, and continued. I did my best, and all went without a hitch. Topper was in best form, and I believed that he, too, knew what was at stake.

On the second day we had the cross-country event. This meant following a course of set jumps – fences and ditches – around an established route away from the event location, with judges standing at each obstacle. At this event too, Topper was, well, tops. He cleared every obstacle easily and as far as I could tell we were back in good time. On the third and last day, showjumping was on the schedule. Topper was a keen jumper and so was I, and we quickly did our round without a single fault.

When all the children in my group had been put through their paces, the judges conferred for a while, and then the results were called out. First, the honourable mentions. And then they announced my ranking: 'In third place, number fifteen, Jo Westmaas on Topper.'

'Jo! You did it! Third place!' cried Lynn. My eyes opened wide with shock and I couldn't say a word.

'Go on, get back on Topper and collect your ribbon,' she said as the winning contestants gathered to once more enter the arena.

The moment I shook the judge's hand, and took the yellow ribbon handed to me, was the proudest in my life to date, and I was the happiest girl in the world. Later, I hugged Topper and nuzzled my face against his neck.

'Thank, you, Topper! You did all the work, really,' I whispered. But I knew it had been teamwork, him and me, and that I had, at long last, mastered a skill.

Chapter Forty-Three

The Best Book in the World

Dear Mum,

I have just finished the book you gave me last Christmas. It is the most beautiful book in the whole world. When I finished it, I cried and cried and cried. I'm going to read it again and again, a million times. Thank you.

I'm really sorry about the exeat last term. I have a really bad conscience now. You came all that way and I was so rude. I suppose you must love me to come all that way. I'm sorry I was rude. I love you too.

Love, Jo

Over a year had passed since I'd opened Mum's present to me on that first Christmas in England. I'd matured, and could now understand and cope with some of the adult themes. I opened it again, and this time I persevered. It took a bit of time until I could sink into the story. This was not one of the easy-to-read Enid Blyton books that grabbed you and swept you into the story from the first page. This was a book you had to slowly sink into. A book with atmosphere. A book where adults and their own issues were a part of the story. It needed patience, and the will to absorb the words so that their meaning opened up. And this time I *got* it.

The name of the book was *My Friend Flicka* and the author was Mary O'Hara.

Once I stepped into it, I couldn't let it go. Night and day, I devoured that book. Night and day, I suffered and yearned and wept with the main character. He was a ten-year-old boy named Ken McLaughlin, who didn't fit in, just like I didn't; whose father didn't understand him, just like my mother didn't understand me; as no adult, in fact, understood me. Ken was a dreamer, who dreamed dreams that couldn't be fulfilled, just like my own dreams, and whose imagination ran away with him and took him to far-off places, as mine did. Reading that book, I *became* Ken, that boy with impossible dreams, so out of place.

When Ken fell in love with the wild, untameable filly Flicka on his father's Wyoming ranch, I agonised with him, feeling his father's disapproval in every cell of my body. When Flicka lay in a stream bleeding from terrible barbed-wire wounds, I wept with Ken. When Ken's father strode out in the night, rifle in hand, to put Flicka out of her misery, my heart broke with Ken's. When Ken himself went out to sit in the stream holding Flicka in his arms, when he caught pneumonia and lay in bed too sick to move or to think, his mother wiping his forehead, I nearly died with him. When he listened keenly to hear the final shot of his father's rifle, my heart stretched out to him, and I listened too.

Flicka had a happy ending, but I never forgot the roller-coaster ride of emotions that book took me on. It was the first time I truly learned of the power of the written word, the power of a good and sensitively truthful story. I've been in thrall to that power ever since. It sowed the seed for what I was to eventually become; or rather, it nourished a seed that had been with me right from the start – I was born with it.

*

Meanwhile, at Summer Hill, new prospects were brewing.

'Jo, I've just received a letter from your mother,' said Mrs W. 'She said she'd like to treat us both to a little holiday. You'd like that, wouldn't you?'

I looked at her with shining eyes and nodded vigorously.

'Well then, let's do it. Would you prefer a holiday in winter or in summer?'

What a question! I hated winter, with a capital H. Every time the cold season came around, I dreamed of blue waters, golden sands, and sunshine, sunshine, sunshine. Warm sunshine, not this bleached-out gleam hiding behind dreary grey clouds that passed for fine winter weather so I replied without hesitation: 'Winter!'

'Very well then, I'll organise something for the Christmas holidays.'

And with that cheerful prospect in both our minds, she drove me back to Harrogate.

By now, we girls were all shapes and sizes. We were becoming young women. Some had sprung up tall and thin like beanpoles, some were rounding out, and some were still as small as children. Our ages ranged from twelve, like me, to fourteen, the oldest of our batch. Some had already 'started' their periods, amid much boasting, and many had the soft mounds of growing breasts. Some even wore bras, the envy of all.

Some of us wore skirts. I didn't. The standard uniform for senior school was a lovely dark green tweed skirt with little flecks of red and yellow and light green woven into the fabric. It was an A-line skirt, knee-length, and, in my eyes, quite stylish and very grown-up. They were worn with long-sleeved white shirts and green neckties striped with your house colour – in my case, light blue – and a green cardigan. This smart uniform made you look very adult. Some girls in my year had already outgrown their silly straight-up-and-down tunics and were already wearing those skirts. Others, like me, still had the bodies of children, and Forsyth's of Glasgow simply did not have them in our sizes. But we grew, filled out, and one by one, the smallest girls progressed to tweed skirts. I was the last. There I was, still in my Oakdale tunic, wishing and waiting to become a real woman, as evidenced by a skirt.

But finally, my tomboy days were over for good. At last I too shot up and filled out, and was able to proudly progress to a skirt. It was to be years, though, before I grew breasts and got my period. Impatient to become a *proper* girl, I yearned for these signs of womanhood: how could I not? Growing up was the hippest thing around. I couldn't wait. There, right before my eyes, were all these wonderful, brilliant, funny, delightful girls, or young women, and I wanted nothing more than to finally belong to their ranks.

Chapter Forty-Four

Smuts

Dear Mum,

Have you ever heard of The Beatles? They are absolutely fab. I love them. My favourite is George.

Love, Jo

Over that summer, unbeknownst to me, a phenomenon had swept through Britain and the world. I hadn't known before now because Mrs W. did not have television. But now, back at school, we did. My form, the Lower Fourth, shared the Junior Common Room – the Junior Comm – in Lincoln House – East and West combined – with the Upper Fourth, and most of the girls were already switched on. Nobody, of course, knew that we were witnessing the greatest shift in popular culture since Elvis Presley. Greater, actually, than Elvis, and he'd been huge enough.

In February of that year, a song by an unknown pop group had hit Number Two in the *Top of the Pops* charts. That song was 'Please Please Me', and the name of the group was The Beatles. Later that year, in April, a song called 'From Me to You' by the same group hit Number One in the charts.

Now, with all of us gathered in the Junior Common Room – the Junior Comm – on a Wednesday night for *Top of the Pops*, it happened. History was being made, and we in that Junior Comm were all witnesses. On that day, 18 September 1963, 'She Loves You' hit Number One. The Junior Comm exploded in an ecstasy beyond description. Some of us swooned. Some of us wept. Some of us – well, what the other girls felt I obviously don't know, but for me it was like being swept up in a wave of sheer unadulterated adoration. That song touched every nerve, every lost and lonely atom of my being. I too rode that wave: we all did. We didn't know it then, but we were part of a movement, united in the collective hysteria of young girls on the brink of adolescence. There was a name for it: Beatlemania.

From that day on we were all in thrall to The Beatles, and that was just the beginning of a devotion that had no end. Soon we were able to identify them all, those mop-headed, outrageously pretty young men in their shiny black suits. We learned their names. We knew who played which guitar – bass: Paul, rhythm: John, lead: George – and who played drums – Ringo. We each had a favourite. Paul was by far the most popular. I adored them all but, not wanting to go with the crowd, I chose George as my beloved. We learned that only John was married. We learned how they'd started out, in the Cavern Club. We were in love, most of us for the first time, and hopelessly so. And there was to be no recovery, because month after month, they produced one hit after another, and as each song hit the Number One spot, the more we knew this was the love affair of a lifetime. Through the months, the years ahead, we were hopelessly, un-redeemably hooked.

The rumours had been right. It was time for The Talk. We'd been whispering, giggling about it for ages, especially at Lights Out. Many of us actually already knew the embarrassing details, thanks to a certain assistant matron from Oakdale who smuggled forbidden books to us, or from our mothers. My own mother had written me a letter telling me all about the Facts of Life in a matter-of-fact and completely objective manner. So I knew. Most of us did. It was the fact that Miss Todd, that venerable, awe-inspiring, dignified grey-haired woman who led the chapel services as well as assembly, was going to be the one to open that box containing the epitome of intimate adult mysteries: well, we couldn't wait, and who could blame us? Tittering behind hands, eyes sparkling with mirth, we gathered in the assigned room and waited for her to arrive. At last she did.

The Talk, when it finally came, was supremely disappointing. The high point was when she told us about our 'private parts': 'You know why they're called private parts, don't you? Because they're private!' And that, for me, was the essence of The Talk. Nothing at all titillating or risqué or, God forbid, containing actual graphic detail of the dramatic acts we would all one day have to deal with. But there was a lot about pregnancy and motherhood. 'That was *it*?' some of us asked each other when it was over. And yes, that was it: a helpless and awkward avoidance of detail. And yet, it was enough. A snippet of wisdom that served me well for the rest of my life.

One thing was clear: it was high time we all fell in love. We'd already fallen in love with one Beatle or another, but we needed proper, visible, physical, living objects of our adoration – or rather, victims. That's where 'smuts' made their entrance.

Smuts were older girls of the Lower Fifth. As the middle level between juniors and seniors, the Lower Fifth had a special status and, in Lincoln at least, their own Comm, known as the LV Comm. Aged between fourteen and fifteen, they were proper little women: not yet adults but children no more, and still accessible to us, unlike the haughty seniors.

The deal was that us Lower Fourthers had to pick a Lower Fifther, and that was our smut. You diverted all your frayed feelings of unrequited love, all those emotional loose ends, to this girl. You adored her, whether she responded or not. You served her.

You cleaned her shoes and carried her books across to school. You drew pictures for her, and wrote her little love notes. You tidied her lockers. You were simply *there* for her.

I was late in choosing my smut, but eventually I settled on a girl with short dark hair who went by the nickname Clocky, short for her surname McLaughlin. Perhaps I picked her because that surname was reminiscent of Ken McLaughlin, the boy in the Flicka books I so identified with, but there may very well have been other reasons.

There was certainly no particular rapport between us but, over time, much later and after several similar episodes, I learned something very important. A lesson in love, and loving. Through this exercise of pining love for a person, I learned that loving is an act of will. That love is a decision. It comes from within the Lover, not the Beloved. The Lover can bestow it, and withdraw it. Love, of the capital-L kind, remains the same, for its source is within, inexhaustible, and never-ending. Once bestowed, it can be nourished, and if reciprocated, it can grow into a magnificent and solid edifice. But always, its source is within: an endless reservoir we hold in our hearts.

And I loved Clocky. I really did. It was love at a distance, as I was far too much in awe of her ever to actually *talk* to her. And it was plainly unrequited. But I showed her my love in every way I could. Not knowing who her favourite Beatle was, I drew her pictures of George Harrison and once or twice carried her books over to school for her. She pointedly ignored my attentions. I wasn't hurt. You simply had to love, whether or not that love was returned. I developed a most sublime understanding of the meaning of the word love. Sometimes, it simply meant pining away, because there was never a guarantee of the ultimate reward: being loved back. Loving had to be its own reward; you couldn't demand a response.

*

Sometime later in the year Miss Todd gave us a lecture in which she strictly forbade the tradition of smutting. She didn't give a reason. And that was the end of Clocky and me. It was a painless parting. But I never regarded the love I'd felt as any less just because it had been ended so easily, on command. It had been real while it lasted, and that was the main thing.

Chapter Forty-Five

Haus in Der Sonne

Dear Mum,

I can't believe you're sending me to Austria. To the ice and snow! Why? You know I hate the cold. I'm going to hate it there! I hate winter! When I said winter holiday, I meant the Caribbean! I want sunshine and blue skies and the warm lapping sea! How could you send me on a skiing trip! It's awful!

Love, Jo

'It's going to be a lovely holiday, Jo! We're going to Austria! You'll learn to ski!'

I gasped aloud in shock. Austria! Skiing! Snow! *Winter!*

She thought it was a gasp of joy, but it was the opposite. Alas, Mrs W. had completely misunderstood my answer to her question. Yes, I'd chosen winter for our holiday, but not a *winter sport* holiday! That was the last thing on my mind! That was *terrible!* I wanted warmth, sunshine, *a beach!* It didn't even have to be a Caribbean beach – just any warm, sunny place away from the cold and greyness of an English winter.

But I said nothing. Mrs W., unaware of my deep disappointment, set about packing our suitcases and one morning, off we went,

Lynn driving us to Manchester Airport. Mrs W.'s best friend, who was called Joan just like her, was coming with us, so our names were Joan, Joan, and Jo, which Mrs W. and Joan liked to joke about.

After landing at Basel Airport we took a train through Switzerland to Austria, and there began a truly fairy-tale journey. That train passed through the most magnificent landscape I'd seen in my life. I sat glued to the window, completely mesmerised. Yes, everything was covered in the cold white stuff, but it was so out-of-this-world beautiful. I watched spellbound as we sped north-eastwards to Austria, finally forced to revoke my hatred of winter. I declared, to myself, Switzerland as the most beautiful country on earth, because nothing could surpass this: those magnificent snow-covered mountains etched against a brilliant blue sky, sun sparkling on tree-skeletons outlined in glistening white, fairy-tale villages as if from a different era, mountainsides sprinkled with adorable wooden chalets and smoking chimneys bestowing the promise of cosy interiors.

It was an all-day journey but finally, in the late afternoon, we arrived at the station in Schruns. From there we took a bus to our final destination, a village in the Vorarlberg Mountains called Gaschurn. And finally, we arrived at our hotel, which was called Haus in der Sonne. I didn't know any German as yet, but it was easy to guess what that meant. And so, at least in name, I would have my sun.

The hotel was made of wood through and through, but was completely different to our colonial-style wooden houses in Georgetown, which were traditionally painted pristine white inside and out, sometimes with green touches on window-shutters or banisters. This house was made of solid wood. The floors, walls and ceilings were all made of sturdy timber, transparently stained to reveal the actual grain and character of the logs or planks. The walls seemed to be of whole logs, solid squared-off tree-trunks, some horizontal, some vertical, all polished brown. Inset into one of the walls was a large black stove with a glass window through which you could see the fire burning within it. It gave off a deliciously cosy warmth that filled the whole room. I soon learned the name for this contraption: *Kachelofen.*

In fact, I very soon learned a whole lot more German words. In a few days I could count to a hundred in German, and ask for the translation-dictionary – *darf ich bitte das Lexikon haben?'* – as well as, of course, *Guten Morgen, Gute Nacht, Guten Tag* and *Auf Wiedersehen.*

It was a small, cosy hotel, quite central, the same as all the other wooden houses on its street. There were few guests. Mrs W. had booked me a bedroom of my own, for which I was grateful – I'd been terrified I'd have to share one with her. The central room had a long dining table set against one of the walls where all of the guests ate together. I had been looking forward to this mysterious thing I'd heard about from the girls at school, all of whom seemed to enjoy frequent holidays on 'the Continent'. The thing was the renowned Continental Breakfast. I'd imagined something rather stupendous, and so great was my disappointment on finding out it was nothing more than bread slices or rolls with slices of cheese, ham or jam. And, of course, butter.

'Fresh butter! From local Swiss cows!' rejoiced Mrs W., but I was little impressed. The milk, though, fresh too, was quite delicious. Boiled or fried eggs were available on request, but no cornflakes, which was my preferred breakfast. Never mind. Down with it all, because it was my first day in Gaschurn and soon after breakfast it was out to the slopes, and Mrs W. had booked skiing lessons for us all.

I was in a children's beginner group on the gentle slopes. I put away my original reluctant prejudice and applied myself to learning to ski: sidling up the slope, whooshing down again. To my surprise it all turned out to be quite enjoyable, but not nearly as much as riding. I knew then and there that this was my first and last skiing holiday. As beautiful as the mountains were, the whole rigmarole was not for me. I wanted to be at home and sit curled up by the *Kachelofen* reading one of the books I'd brought. I was now absorbed by the sequels to *My Friend Flicka, Thunderhead* and *Green Grass of Wyoming.*

On the slopes of Gaschurn, winter 1963–64

I hadn't realised it, but it seems word had spread about me. Again, I hadn't even realised I was different to everyone else. Or rather, I *wasn't* different, but I *looked* different. The children of Gaschurn must have decided among themselves that I needed to be informed of how terrible it was to look different, because one afternoon, on my way home alone from the slopes, they gathered, about twenty of them – or maybe it just seemed like twenty or more, I didn't count. I just know that I was suddenly the centre of a circle of children, all chanting: *'Negerlein! Negerlein! Negerlein!'*

Once again, I didn't need a translation. I already knew that the suffix *-lein* is a diminutive. So I was a little one of those N's.

It was a shock to my system that I never forgot, and never quite forgave, although perhaps I should. I must have been the first properly dark-skinned person they'd seen in their lives, the first to invade their little sheltered village in the snowy mountains. The tourists who came there were invariably white. I was an exotic anomaly, sticking out like a sore thumb. They'd probably only seen pictures in their geography books, or maybe on TV and in films – if they even ever went to the cinema – of people like me. But it had been the same in Cumberland, and no children had taken it into their heads there to gather round me and chant out their amazement. It was the same at school: I stuck out like a sore thumb there too, as I later realised from the school photos of classes or houses or the whole school. No English children had ever mocked me.

This was sheer ignorance, combined with unbridled rudeness. The English, the more refined ones at least, might have been just as ignorant or unused to people of a different race, but were fundamentally far too polite to ever make a scene about it. And for that, I am grateful. And yes, I know this is not the case for everyone with dark skin. I know that some of us have faced and still face horrific abuse and treatment in the United Kingdom. Speaking only for myself as a child, I was spared such treatment. But not in Austria. There, I was subjected to the full blast of that insidious combination of ignorance and contempt.

But the blood of my parents ran through my veins. I stood there until they'd finished their chant and drifted away so I could pass, and then I continued on my way home, skis over my shoulder. 'Stupid idiots!' I thought to myself, and that was that. There are stupid idiots in all times and all countries, and they come in all shapes and sizes and colours.

But I never forgot *those* particular stupid idiots. I wonder where they are now, as adults around my own age. I wonder if they remember me and, in this more enlightened age, feel embarrassment and guilt.

Chapter Forty-Six

Bellum Bellum Bellum

Dear Mum,

The Austria holiday was awful but it was also good, in a way. But I never want to go skiing again. I really, really hate winter. I hate white Christmases. I just want to bask in the sun when December comes. I don't belong with all these white people. They know it, too.

Love, Jo

Back at school, I decided to take up German as an extra-curricular subject. After all, I'd had a bit of a grounding and I'd enjoyed what I'd learned to date. I'd always loved new languages. Languages, I found, opened doors to new cultures. Each new foreign language was a bridge to a different world. I loved the sound of French, and took pleasure in understanding songs and texts in that language. Every year, in the run-up to Christmas, we'd all learn Christmas carols in a variety of languages: not only French, but Spanish and Italian and even Icelandic. I'd loved that.

I was eager to add German to my repertoire. I'd loved the German carols they'd sung on Christmas Eve at Haus in der Sonne, and I wanted to know this language. It was so delightfully logical in a way English was not, and it was an interesting challenge, learning not only the names of nouns but their genders too – three! – and to decipher the appropriate pronouns and adjectives that change according to the noun's gender as well as its grammatical case.

There were two other girls in beginners' German class at HLC. Unfortunately, I did not like the teacher at all. She was a German woman who was stiff and formal, rendering any connection impossible. I dropped German after one term. But languages were my forte. Words could open worlds, and the more languages I knew, the more bridges I could cross into different worlds.

Latin was now compulsory and I'd made a fantastic start last term. Even before the first Latin class, we'd all chanted: *blum blum blum, blee blo blo, bla bla bla, blorum bliss bliss*: the gender declension of *bellum*, war.

I was very good at Latin. At our first exam, at the end of the Christmas term, I'd passed the exam with 99 per cent, just one mark short of perfect. Unfortunately though, one girl, Caroline, got 100 per cent and so it was she, not I, who came first in class. But then, Caroline was annoyingly brilliant and had been so even back at Oakdale. She always came first in everything, and was continuing in that exasperating vein now at senior school. Always the best, in every subject – even maths, my particular bugbear. She wore glasses too, which only emphasised her brilliance. She was one of those girls who'd definitely go on to Oxford or Cambridge and would have a dazzling career in law or medicine, sailing through school on a raft provided by doting parents.

We had moved on from the arithmetic of Oakdale to proper mathematics, which included algebra and geometry, all as separate subjects. I proved to be mediocre at arithmetic and hopeless at algebra, but brilliant at geometry. Accordingly, I loved geometry, hated algebra and tolerated arithmetic. I didn't like the maths teacher, which made matters worse. Invariably my performance in every subject was linked to how well the teacher taught it, or how much I liked her. Unfortunately, I did not like Miss Brock, the

Latin teacher, and though I loved the subject at first, by the end of that school year my exam mark had fallen to only 70 per cent.

Classes were streamed at senior school, and I was in the A stream, which was the best. But I was not one of those gifted pupils who were all-rounders, such as Caroline. We were loosely separated into arts pupils and science pupils, and she was both. I was without doubt an arts pupil: good at languages, English Language, English Literature and, of course, art. I still wrote good essays and one of my favourite exercises was précis, in which we were given a longish text and had to reduce it to a fraction of its length while retaining the pertinent points. I was very good at this, and it proved useful for my later work as a journalist and, much later, a novelist.

That year our English teacher gave us the task of creating magazines ourselves. She divided us into groups and chose an editor for each group. I was editor for my group. I could choose the theme of my magazine and the title, and assign tasks to each of my journalists. It goes without saying that my theme was 'horses'; and the name of my mag was *Tally-Ho!* The previous year I'd taken part in a fox hunt up in Cumberland, with The Commander as Master. I'd ridden Topper. It had been great fun, all that charging around the countryside at the rear of the streaming horses and racing hounds, but the poor foxes! Luckily, they didn't catch one that time.

Tally-ho! wasn't limited to fox-hunting, and luckily some of my journalists had ponies at home and so provided good copy for my fledgling magazine. *Tally-ho!* won first prize, my greatest achievement at Harrogate.

Like maths, the sciences were a mixed bag for me. We were to take one science subject per term that Lower Fourth year, beginning with physics – which I loved – then moving on to chemistry and finally, biology. I would have loved biology too, if it hadn't been for the fact that it began with botany and photosynthesis, which I found only vaguely interesting. I would have loved human biology.

'Bilge', as we called biology, contained mysteries I was longing to crack, and all because of the Pickle-Baby.

The Pickle-Baby was kept under lock and key in a cupboard in the biology lab. It was a foetus preserved in a large jar. We weren't allowed to see it yet, but one of the seniors who had access somehow managed to get us into the lab and open that cupboard. And there it was.

The Pickle-Baby had tiny legs with feet and toes, and minuscule arms, hands and fingers. Its skin was transparent, its eyes were closed, and its head was bent down. It was the most fascinating thing I'd ever seen. So this was how I'd started out, in Mum's tummy! This was how every human on earth started out! This was what I'd probably shelter one future day in my own tummy, growing a tiny being until it became a full-grown baby, ready to be born. But who was this particular baby? What happened for it to end up in a jar in a school's biology lab? What person would it have become, had it lived? I could have stared at that Pickle-Baby all day long. But it was to be just a short-lived glimpse into one of the greatest mysteries on earth: the gestation of a new human being.

So much for sciences. They were fascinating up to a degree, but in the end, I remained what I'd always been: a dedicated arts person, for whom imagination and the beauty of the worlds that words could unfold were more relevant than Bunsen burners and test-tubes. And here at senior school, we were moving into serious literary realms. It was Shakespeare time.

Each term, we tackled a new play. In the four terms between Christmas term 1963 and Christmas term 1964, our four plays were *A Midsummer Night's Dream*, *As You Like It*, *Julius Caesar* and *The Merchant of Venice*. And as always, studying Shakespeare meant learning certain soliloquies by heart. You had to carve them so deeply into your mind that even fifty years later you would only need a first-line nudge to remember what follows after 'The quality of mercy is not strained' or 'Friends, Romans, countrymen'. I still shudder with pleasure at such a perfect alignment of words.

It turned out that I had more affinity with tragedies than comedies, perhaps a throwback to the silent and serious side of me that became more and more buried under the weight of intellectual knowledge. That still, small voice that had wondered with such intensity *why*? And *wherefore*? And *who*?

Just as at Oakdale, every day began with a short service in the school chapel, with a long service on Sundays. I was still enthralled by the choir, those green-robed figures slowly and solemnly walking up the aisle and taking up their places in the pews left and right of the pulpit. They still gave me goose-bumps, as did their mesmerising renditions of the Te Deum and the Magnificat.

Every Sunday after chapel, we were tasked with learning a prayer and a collect by heart, after which we were tested by a house prefect. If you didn't get it the first time, you had to try and try again until you did get it so it was better, in order to save time, to get it right first time. Personally, I preferred making up my own prayers, to discuss personal matters with God in my own words, and in silence. I'd never been one for sticking to pre-formulated supplications. A little seed of rebellion may have been sown at this time. The question of God still burned within me, but had, for the time being, taken a back seat, behind The Beatles and ponies. The greatest enigma of all was I myself, and by now, I was on the cusp of solving it.

Chapter Forty-Seven

A Hard Day's Night

Dear Mum,

*Dad wrote to me to say he is coming to England with Faye,
Nigel and Gary, and Faye is going to have a baby. He is
coming in the summer and I am to spend time with him.
I hope you don't mind.*

Love, Jo

By now, I was gradually losing the religiosity I'd found at Oakdale.
There was just too much going on. Too much learning, too many
activities, too much frivolous and hilarious fun. And too much
hipness. Here at HLC, the strict reins that held us in check at
Oakdale were dropped quite considerably. We weren't controlled
as much and there wasn't the terrifying figure of Killer in the
background. Our housemistress, Miss Linsdale, wasn't half the
dragon of our old head.

Our Lights Out larks and frolics continued as before. There was
the time when we tried to outdo each other in scary stories, one
of which may have scarred me for life. It was a story called 'The
Copper Bowl', and was about an ancient Chinese torture method by
which the victim was tied to the ground and a copper bowl placed
upside down on his tummy, with a rat beneath it. The famished
rat would, eventually, eat its way through the poor man's stomach.

From that story I developed a lifelong horror of rats, even the nice white ones that are kept as pets. I won't go near them, even now.

For a time I had a new best friend, a day girl called Margaret, who lived in Harrogate. Sometimes I visited her at the weekend, when once again I felt that envy of someone who was so firmly rooted in a real home and intact family. For a while, she and I found a rapport grounded in the very same sense of the absurd, an ability to laugh our heads off at things nobody else could understand. We formed a secret society, consisting of just us two, called The Blobs, of which the only rule was discovering new and secret things to laugh at. We had a secret sign, which consisted of the tips of our forefingers and thumbs meeting and moving back and forth like a kind of beak. We found that hilariously funny.

We still had tuckboxes, but here at college we were given jurisdiction over our tuck instead of being handed three sweets a day. It was half a pound every Sunday, and it was up to us to regulate its consumption: eat it all in a day or two, or spread it out over the week. I was a spreader. We could also order our own fruit from a local greengrocer, which was delivered fresh each week, paid for with our own pocket-money.

The summer term of 1964 was glorious. There was lots of sunshine and sitting out on lawns, our summer dresses rolled up and tucked into our knickers. I never went out on exeats any more – Carole and I had drifted irreconcilably apart since the hamster incident – but I didn't mind. Weekends especially were wonderful, and the entire term was underscored by music. The Beatles were rising from strength to strength with one Number One hit after the other: 'I Want to Hold Your Hand', followed by 'Please Please Me', followed by 'All My Loving'. Then came 'Twist and Shout', 'Can't Buy Me Love', 'Do You Want to Know a Secret' and 'Love Me Do'. And it all culminated with 'A Hard Day's Night'.

We avidly followed this development on Wednesday night's *Top of the Pops*, the climax of every week. Each new song was digested and provided soul nourishment until the next. Whoever our favourite Beatle was, we swooned and wept, our emotions wrung dry in the highest echelons of adoration.

This was Beatlemania at its heady height, and we were all Beatlemaniacs: a frenzy that spread like wildfire through Britain's pubescent and prepubescent girls, flinging them into an uncontrollable chaos of emotional ecstasy. Rumour was spreading about a Beatles' film, titled *A Hard Day's Night*, due to be released that summer. Everyone was going to see it, *everyone*.

Except me. I knew for a fact that Mrs W. would never indulge me in such a frivolity. I couldn't even mention it. I would be the only girl returning next term who hadn't seen it. It was utterly heartbreaking.

But then, shortly before the holidays were to begin, Dad wrote to say he was coming to England on long leave, and he'd be picking me up at the end of term.

Dad brought his family with him: his heavily pregnant young wife Faye and their two sons, Nigel, aged six, and Gary, aged four.

'What would you like to do?' Dad asked.

'I want to see *A Hard Day's Night*!' was my answer. What else?

Dad was one of the few parents who accompanied their daughter to a cinema packed with girls between the ages of twelve and fifteen. Perhaps there were a few older, perhaps a few younger. I, at thirteen, was among the youngest.

The film's storyline was basic to the utmost degree. It depicted a day and a half in the life of the mop-headed four, leading up to a televised concert gig. In the film they are constantly running here and there: from their crazed fans and from their manager, who is constantly trying to rein them in. Panic ensues when Ringo

Starr gets arrested and is going to be late for the recording. Paul McCartney's grandfather pops in now and then for comic relief. The Fab Four perform a dozen or so songs.

The bit that overshadowed most of the non-existent plot, however, was the audience. Not the cinema audience, those of us sitting in the darkened room, eyes glued to the screen in silent adulation. No, it was the girls *in* the film, screaming and weeping in frenzy, arms waving in desperation at their heroes, and faces writhing in agony as tears streamed down their faces. You couldn't hear the songs for the screams.

It was at one of those moments that Dad turned to me and whispered in the hushed cinema: 'You can scream too, if you want.'

If I could ever have loved him more, it was at that moment. I smiled to myself and whispered back, 'It's OK.'

Dad whisked me away from school with Faye and the two little boys. We went to Manchester and to Scotland, where Faye had relatives and where she eventually gave birth to their third son, Christopher. Later during that holiday Dad drove me back to Summer Hill, and on the way, he took the opportunity to take me to visit Bruce's Cave, where according to the legend his great hero Robert the Bruce, while hiding in defeat from the enemy army, watched a spider's repeatedly failed attempts to build a web. Eventually the spider succeeded. And once again Dad drummed into me the old adage: *If at first you don't succeed, try, try, try again.*

Dad also filled me in on political events back at home. As a staunch supporter of Chief Minister Cheddi Jagan, he had high hopes that the People's Progressive Party would win the coming general election in December of that year. In pure numbers, the outcome seemed safe. 'But,' he told me, 'Britain doesn't like him and America doesn't like him either. Anything could happen.'

I wasn't particularly interested in politics. I was interested in Home. Something was nagging at me, exacerbated by having Dad and Faye here with me, and talk of family, the Crown Street gang, the places I loved so much. Plus the guilt about my last interaction with Mum.

There is a name for this feeling: homesickness.

Back at Summer Hill, nostalgia for the past was put aside. I was once again whisked up into the heady world of horses: Pony Club, village fairs, treks, and everything else. The Beatles were instantly forgotten, because Mrs W. had a new surprise waiting for me. On my first day back, she asked, 'Jo, how would you like to own your own pony?'

My own pony? A pony, just for me? Why, I'd be just like Ken in *My Friend Flicka*! It was something I could only have dreamed of up to now. After all, with as many ponies as I wanted at my disposal, it would never have occurred to me to have one exclusively for myself. But Mrs W. and Mum had already exchanged letters on the matter, and Mum had green-lighted the idea.

But which one? I had to sadly admit that I had outgrown my little favourite, Topper. My next favourite was Flip, the Arab-Fell mare who, size-wise, was on the cusp between pony and horse. I adored Flip, but knew that she was a league too high for me, being one of Mrs W.'s own personal favourites. Who else?

'I have a suggestion,' said Mrs W. 'What about Pennant?'

Pennant was Flip's daughter. She'd been a little filly when I first came to Summer Hill and was now three years old, the equivalent to me in horse-years. She'd been halter-broken early on, and was a loveable, tame little girl. Lynn had worked her on the lunge, but she wasn't yet saddle-broken.

'Breaking her in to ride can be your task!' said Mrs W. 'Lynn will teach you – you can work together!'

She didn't need to ask again. Pennant became my very own pony. A pony I could love and call my own, and break in for riding, just as Ken had broken Flicka, except that Pennant wasn't an untameable pony from the wilds. She was a lovely black mare with a mane so long and bushy it covered her eyes and hung low beneath her neck, and a gloriously full tail she swished as she walked. Hair a little frizzy and unkempt, just like mine.

I threw myself into the task of training Pennant. Sometimes, I simply stood beside her and hugged her, whispered in her ear, and enjoyed her little nudges of affection. In the meantime, the busy life at Summer Hill continued, and to my joy, near the end of summer Lynn promoted me to ride Flip for dressage at one of the country shows we attended almost every weekend. It was a huge compliment, and I hoped to live up to her trust in me. And indeed, I did. I didn't win a ribbon, this time, but I was placed fourth in the competition.

Jo on Flip. Is that The Commander's horse in the background?

Next year, I thought to myself, it would be me and Pennant.

We would become a team, Pennant and I. I would train her, all by myself, with Lynn's help. She would love me. She'd follow me around like a dog, adoring me. She would be my closest friend.

Her tail would be long and flowing and blow in the wind like a flag as we cantered over hill and dale, rabbits scattering as we came, and we'd swim in the Irish Sea, me clinging to her slippery neck and laughing, one arm waving free. Her hooves would be clean and well-tended, and her huge dark eyes would regard me with adoration. We would be Ken and Flicka, resurrected. I'd practise dressage and showjumping with her and win red ribbons at all the events. And we'd go trekking and trotting across green fields and vanish into the wide blue yonder, and we would become one.

Jo and Pennant, summer 1963

But right now, I could make her my friend. I could win her love, just as Ken had won Flicka's love. Day after day, that summer, I'd go out into the fields and put my arms around her neck and my face against her warm body and close my eyes and breathe in her beautiful horsey smell. I'd brush her until her black coat glowed; I'd comb out the knots in her long mane the way I combed out the knots in my own shock of curls. Me and Pennant. A team.

And then, it was back to school. Off we drove in trusty old Frances, through Giggleswick and Wigglesworth. I never suspected it would be the very last time I'd hear those tired jokes.

Chapter Forty-Eight

And I Love Her

Dear Mum,

All I can say is: I want to come home. Not forever. Just for Christmas.

Love, Jo

It was the first term in the Upper Fourth. The Beatlemania snowball was gathering ever more momentum and substance. 'And I Love Her', soft and sentimental. 'I Feel Fine'. All of these songs were tapping into the deepest wellspring of emotion of a girl on the cusp of womanhood. That deep yearning to be, above all, loved, adored and cherished by someone happy just to hold her hand. Someone who'd buy her diamond rings. Who'd whisper sweet nothings in her ear. Becoming a woman, leaving childhood behind, is a scary moment, but The Beatles' songs reassured her that through it all, he'd be there for her, holding her, loving her. What more did we need? We were at their feet. *I* was at their feet.

But was that true? Was it really The Beatles that I loved, that I cherished? Were they just a mirage? Was the love they professed perhaps not real, but just adolescent wishful thinking? Maybe there was more to this love thing than a baby-faced mop-headed young man with a guitar who held the power to make girls scream. Were we – was I – perhaps seeking something else, something more permanent, more *real*? Could that emotion find another, more perpetual, home? And what about ponies, what about Pennant? Indeed, I loved them. They were the reason for the long path that had taken me from a warm and vibrant home to a chilly and bleak corner of England. All of this, to throw my arms around an animal I loved, but which could not love me back. Was that *all*? Had I found paradise? Was this true love?

For me personally, the question of love had a new dimension, one that made me feel increasingly uncomfortable. Being with Dad during the holidays, our loving and uncomplicated connection had released new feelings in me that I was forced to confront.

I hadn't seen Mum since my awful rebuff of her, back in 1962. She'd never complained, I'd never properly apologised. But it dug into my conscience. There is something inherent within us that knows when we've made a false step, when we've acted against an unspoken code of human relationships, and most so when it concerns parents and children. Something within us knows when we have gone against the law of unconditional love. Even when we push away that still, small voice and refuse to listen, we know. And I knew. I had to put things right, and a letter wouldn't do it.

Something was broken. And I felt it was up to me now to start the process of healing. There were things I needed to understand. Why had I rejected Mum when she came to visit? Why, when I knew that I loved her, had I pushed her away so rudely? Why had the connection with her never really worked out? Why, in all our closeness, were we so distant? Had I wounded her, beyond repair? Could I make it all good again?

I wanted to go home. Just for a holiday. A holiday in the sunshine. Christmas, at home, with all those wonderful fuzzy sensations, that feeling of being wrapped in a warm cloak, infused with music that struck secret chords in the very depths of my being. Sentimental, yes, but no less powerful, and when absent,

replaced by a deep and lastir.
all, I wanted to see Mum, hug
up for what had happened two ye
without a second thought.

I didn't try to analyse it. I was st
this deep longing. Along with the in
of guilt. I hadn't thanked her, ever. N
spending and spending, all for me. She
compensation money from the West Indies
all she had in savings. She'd sent me to an
could never have afforded had she not come ii
windfall years ago. She'd given me opportunitie
my family background could only dream about. S
wildest dreams of horses and riding. She'd sent n
sport holiday. And to cap it all, she'd bought me a pon
And all without ever a word of complaint or an appe.
say one word of thanks. A word I'd never spoken. I'd tak
granted, and now it all came back to me with alarming int

I *needed* to see her. I needed to say thank you. And so.
person. I needed to go home. Just for Christmas.

Could I even ask for that, a return flight all the way to Brit.
Guiana? More expenses, more organisation? I wrote to her, beggin
her to let me come.

She complied of course. When had she ever denied me anything
I'd set my heart on?

She booked my ticket. Of course she did.

In mid-December of that year, another Universal Aunt put me
on a BOAC flight bound for Georgetown, once again as an unaccompanied minor, cared for by a stewardess. Arriving at Atkinson
Field, I stepped down the landing stairs into the sunshine, and
that familiar feeling of well-being rose up in me: I was home.

g through immigration, I walked into the arrivals hall
BOAC hostess in charge and looked around for Mum.
sn't there. I could have cried.

Leila had come with a taxi to pick me up. 'Mummy
make it, dear,' she said as she hugged me. 'Parliament is
today and she had to work. By the time we get home,
, she'll be back.'

ad to contain myself.

the way down to Georgetown that inimitable sensation of
ing home flooded through me. The ramshackle villages we passed
rough with little wooden houses balanced precariously on high
ooden stilts, dray-carts holding up traffic, as well as the occasional
tray dog or vagrant cow crossing the potholed road. The taxi-driver,
yelling through the open window at a careless overtaker: 'Hey! You
got your licence on a donkey-cart or what?' Passing Diamond Sugar
Estate with that overpowering sweetly-sickly smell of fermented
sugar. And then, finally, the town. The Public Buildings, where
Mum worked. Stabroek Market. St George's Cathedral. Down the
tree-lined avenue of Main Street, the flamboyant trees all red with
Christmas flowers. And at last, Lamaha Street.

My heart hammering crazily, I walked up the outside stairs to
the front door and plunged into the drawing room. Mum had
been upstairs in the bedroom, waiting for me. Now I saw her,
coming down the stairs, her face wreathed in smiles. What else
could I do? I lunged forward, threw myself into her arms. They
closed around me.

I was home.

That was the most delightful Christmas of all. Here I was,
back where I belonged. There was that old nostalgic feeling of

Christmas wrapped around me, drawing me into a comfort that had been buried for all those years in England. Oakdale School, Harrogate College, Summer Hill, even Pennant; they all faded into insignificance in that cushion of cosy delight. And just as stars fade at the rising of the sun, I knew I had truly come home.

George Harrison. Clocky. Pennant. I'd loved them all, given them my heart. In each case, I'd thought it was a forever-love. Such is the easily ignited euphoria of youth, the capacity to surrender completely to evanescent emotions. However real they seemed at the time, they were, ultimately, fleeting. Untethered, I'd leapt from one love-anchor to the next in a forlorn quest for *home*. Home, in the truest sense of the word: love, strong and permanent. And I knew now that the greatest love came through her: a love as true as gold.

This was where I belonged, and where I had always belonged. I belonged with Mum, and always had. She was my source of all that was good in the world. Love was all I needed, and her love was the best of all. Better than The Beatles. Better even than Pennant. Not better than God's love, but surely it was God's love that flowed through her. She was a conduit, and now, cushioned in that special joy of Christmas, I felt it, deeper than I'd ever done before.

Perhaps it's true that absence makes the heart grow fonder. Perhaps it's true that you only know what you truly love when you no longer have it. The years in England had been essential for a number of reasons: for finding my independence and my skills, for finding a deep stability within myself, for initiating a search for God that was to last a lifetime. But most of all it brought into stark relief, hidden for years until now, back home, what was more obvious than anything else: she was, and always had been, the centre of my universe. And England was no longer necessary.

Sometime after New Year, I said to her: 'I don't want to go back to England.'

'But you're doing so well at school! And what about your pony? Pennant?' she said.

I shook my head. 'It all doesn't matter. I don't care about Pennant. I don't care about school. I want to stay here. With you.'

And stay I did, with one last little detail: 'Mum, I want to be called Sharon again now.'

And from that day forth, I was.

Epilogue

Home Again

Mum registered me for Bishops' High School, her old alma mater. This was the school where her brilliant performances and stellar behaviour had culminated in her being head girl for her final year.

As such, lofty expectations were placed on me from the beginning. The present headmistress, Miss Lilian Dewer, had been just a year or two above Mum and knew her well. 'You have a lot to live up to, Sharon!' she warned me. From the start, I was aware of the size of the footsteps I was expected to follow in. It soon emerged that Bishops' High School was even stricter than Oakdale.

Needless to say, and true to a developing character of reckless abandonment, I chose to go in the opposite direction to both Mum's example and Bishops' rules. How could it be otherwise? I was like a filly let loose in the open plains of Wyoming after years of dressage training in a closed English manège. I tossed my head, flung out my hooves, and careened through life enjoying my new-found freedom.

On my insistence, Mum and I moved into her own house in Subryanville, just a minute from the sea, and that house became a hub of teenage activity. I reaped the highest praise and envy from my friends for having the most liberal-minded parent in town, who placed no restrictions on me.

By now there was a Pony Club in Georgetown where you could hire mounts to ride, and there I met my first best friend, Margaret, the daughter of an Indian doctor whose name had been changed on the whim of an English immigration officer from something unpronounceable to him – probably Tamil – to Kerry. I didn't have my own pony, but Margaret did, a gelding called Vitane. She and I clattered through the streets of Georgetown or galloped along the beach, and, in the years following, in our free time painted the town red.

And then I teamed up with my classmate, Pratima Nath, the daughter of a very strict Hindu father who was a first-generation Indian immigrant. What fun it was, evading his edicts! We were young, we were free, we were hip. The world was ours to conquer, and conquer it we did.

And the rest is history.

The End of Oakdale

Oakdale is sadly no more.

In the late sixties, the governors decided that the increasing costs of upkeep of both the building and the grounds were no longer financially feasible; furthermore, the older girls needed access to more senior subjects. In 1968 the school was closed; the girls were transferred to a house in the main building. Miss Killingley and her staff went with them. The girls moved on: but what about that lovely building, so jaw-droppingly beautiful to me when I first arrived? Well, that's a story in itself.

After it was put up for sale, a wealthy businessman bought it in 1970. He originally wanted to extend it for conversion into small hotel, but, like so many of us, he fell in love with the premises and decided instead to convert it into a private residence. He spent a small fortune on renovations and additions, including a swimming pool. However, for reasons known only to himself, after a few years everything went pear-shaped. He simply vanished. The building stood vacant for a while, but then, vandals moved in, and trashed it so completely that it could not be saved.

A property developer took over, and planned to demolish it and build twelve detached houses in that idyllic location. But it was a listed building and could not be pulled down without permission.

In her book *Harrogate College 1893–1973*, the deputy head-mistress Dorothy Hewlett (known to us girls as Booey) tells the sad story of what happened next. *'It was at this point,'* she writes, *'that preservation societies belatedly entered the fray, and after heated argument the matter was referred to the Ministry of the Environment. As a result of the inquiry the Ministry ruled, because of the state of the dilapidation, in favour of demolition.'* The whole building was razed to the ground, reduced to vast piles of rubble, *'and so it has remained since,'* according to Miss Hewlett. *'The beck still flows undisturbed and the daffodils have given their annual display but the rest is desolation.'*

In more recent years, a housing development was erected on the land.

I can only join with Miss Hewlett in her reminiscences: *'there were some special occasions at Oakdale that no-one who has been there could forget.' She* recalls the summer evenings with the pets – rabbits, guinea pigs and hamsters – scampering across the lawn. The fireworks out in the eerie darkness of Guy Fawkes night, the huge bonfire. The wonder and mystery of the Nativity Play, in which everyone took part. The sheer magic of the Christmas party, conjuror included. Oakdale under snow. The bubbling beck – '… *all part of the life that was Oakdale, and all now tucked away as memories.'*

As we, the last of the old girls, age, our memories will fade ever more. I write this on my seventieth birthday, and hope that with this book I can not only revive some of those memories but also invite others into the life that was once Oakdale.

A Letter from Sharon

Thank you! Thank you for coming along with me on this journey through my childhood; I do hope you've enjoyed the read. There's no doubt I had an unusual upbringing, unusual parents, and my hope is that you, the reader, have enjoyed this journey into my quirky past. If so, I'd be very grateful if you'd pass the word on to your friends, family and social media contacts, and perhaps write a review to share your impressions with other readers. And, if you want to discover more inspiring memoirs, just sign up at the following link. Your email address will never be shared, and you can unsubscribe at any time.

www.thread-books.com/sign-up

For me, writing this has been a fascinating journey back into the past, as memories I'd thought long forgotten popped back into clear perspective; names and situations that had been buried rose into daylight.

Other memories are, of course, too deep to rise, for they are shrouded in the darkness of early babyhood. To reconstruct these, I've had to rely on information told me by my parents and other relatives who were adults at the time, the vast majority of whom have now passed on. Sometimes, memories have tumbled back into focus, as alive as ever; some have made me laugh, some have made me cry, and I've bathed in the sweet solace of nostalgia. Those were, indeed, the days! Never to return, but still a source of much joy. What a great opportunity to reminiscence!

Some memories have made me question myself; some have forced me to better understand the child I once was, and the dynamics behind my sometimes strange responses, back then, to people and situations; how those responses contribute to the woman I grew up to be today. They have also forced me to better understand the major players in my life; first and foremost, of course, my mother and father. It's all about perspective; the long lens of time has brought not only deeper love and understanding but compassion and, where needed, closure.

You're welcome to stay in touch through Facebook, Twitter, Goodreads or the contact form on my website. I'd love to hear from you, and promise to reply.

Sharon

sharonmaasauthor

@sharon_maas

www.sharonmaas.com

Acknowledgements

Writing a memoir wasn't as easy as I'd first thought. I write fiction, twelve novels to date, and, being a basically introverted person (as you have found out in this memoir!) who is private in the extreme, writing this has forced me to 'get over myself': a good thing. I suppose it all began with my last novel, *The Far Away Girl*, which was about a little girl growing up in Guyana; that's the book that threw my past into my face, tossed me into the rabbit-hole of memory, and forced me to dig it all up. I have a life story worth telling, and inhibition and silence is nothing but self-indulgence. As Mum would say, get over it! *Talk!*

Mum is no longer with us; she passed away in 2014, at the ripe old age of ninety-six. I happened to be with her at the time; she wisely chose my yearly two-week visit to Guyana to depart this world – though I did have to extend that trip, to take care of the sad aftermath. She gave me life; she gave me love. She gave me all she had. I owe my sense of independence, of thinking for myself and not simply slotting my opinions and values and attitudes – my whole perspective on life – into the mainstream mould, to her. She gave me the freedom to take risks, to have adventures; she did this in ways few parents would be capable of. And so posthumous and very public thanks go to her.

The same, but from a different aspect, to Dad. He was the one who from the very start, even before I could read and reason myself, made sure that my values were good ones; that compassion and caring for others were part of my repertoire of qualities to strive for. His rather clichéd life maxims (today they would be called memes) worked; they have stayed with me all my life: *If at first you don't succeed, try, try, try again! The love of money is the root of all evil! Power corrupts; absolute power corrupts absolutely!* It was he who taught me not to worship wealth, power, status, material objects; and though a confirmed atheist himself, it was he who, unawares, set me on a quest for spirituality that was to last my entire life. A thoroughly good man, who, like Mum, taught me by living example what human goodness means.

A few people were able to fill in some of the gaps in my family history: my cousins Rod Westmaas and Ron Westmaas, as well as, from my mother's side, Michael Wight and Gale Ramsammy. Thanks to the four of you! Other snippets of information came from Maggie Cheek (formerly Margaret Foreman) as well as Caroline Hunter, who provided information on her mother, Winnie Hunter, and the story of St Margaret's School. Thanks, too, to some of the old girls of Harrogate Ladies' College in the school's alumnae group on Facebook; it is such fun, picking each other's brains for schoolday memories.

Thanks too to Lynn Richardson, who I was able to locate with the help of social media: you played a major role in my coming of age, and it was so good to revisit those days and bring them to life! Thanks too to her granddaughter Emily Richardson for her kind help in the final pre-publication stages. Hopefully I can visit you both soon, and revive my memories of that lovely part of England!

As for the actual writing of this book: my extraordinary editor Claire Bord is deserving of enormous amounts of praise. Claire's constant trust and encouragement and editorial skill were what helped me to dig ever deeper, to structure and sculpt this book to make it as good as it can be.

And of course, behind the scenes the busy staff of Bookouture, who in this year of Covid-19 were all working from home, did the rest to bring it up to scratch and help it go out in the world:

Jacqui Lewis, Jane Donovan, Sarah Whittaker. Last but not least, my thanks to the Thread team, including Nina Winters, Myrto Kalavrezou, Alex Crow, Melanie Price and Occy Carr, on their work in bringing it out to my readers.

And last of all, thanks to my family: daughter Saskia, son Miro, son-in-law Tony, for their abiding support. I couldn't do it without you lot!

Printed in Great Britain
by Amazon